KEYS TO VICTORIOUS LIVING

A WORKBOOK FOR BELIEVERS

VICTOR D'MONTE

Keys to Victorious Living
By Victor D'Monte

© 2018 Victor D'Monte

First Edition 2018
ISBN-9781791321543

All rights reserved.
No part of this publication may be reproduced, stored in a retrieval system, or transmitted in any form or by any means, electronic, mechanical, photocopying, recording or otherwise, without the prior permission of the publisher, except in the case of brief quotations embodied in critical reviews and certain other noncommercial uses permitted by copyright law. For permission requests, write to the publisher, addressed "Attention: Permissions Co-ordinator," at the address below.

#14, Adonai Church, Heerachand Road, Cox Town, Bangalore - 560005

Most of the Scripture quotations, unless otherwise indicated, are taken from the NEW KING JAMES VERSION of the Bible. Copyright © 1980 by Thomas Nelson, Inc.

Scripture quotations marked NIV are taken from the HOLY BIBLE, NEW INTERNATIONAL BIBLE ® NIV ®

Scripture quotations marked AMP are taken from the AMPLIFIED BIBLE ©

Scripture quotations marked AMPC are taken from the AMPLIFIED BIBLE. CLASSIC EDITION ©

Scripture quotations marked ESV are taken from the ENGLISH STANDARD VERSION © of the Bible.

Scripture quotations marked KJV are taken from the KING JAMES VERSION © of the Bible.

Scripture quotations marked ISV are taken from the INTERNATIONAL STANDARD VERSION © of the Bible.

Scripture quotations marked MSG are taken from THE MESSAGE © Version of the Bible.

The Hebrew and Greek meanings of words used in this book are taken from the Strong's Exhaustive Concordance ©

Cover and Book Design: Thomas Charles

Imprint
Any brand names and product names mentioned in this bookmark subject to trademark, brand or patent protection and are trademarks or registered trademarks of their respective holders. The use of brand names, product names, common names, trade names, product description, etc. even without a particular marking in this work is in no way to be construed to mean that such names may be regarded as unrestricted in respect of trademark and brand protection legislation and could thus be used by anyone.

DEDICATION

I dedicate *'Keys to Victorious Living'* to all those who have just discovered their new found joy and hope in Jesus their Saviour.

I sincerely trust this workbook will enable you to walk in victory and live the life of an overcomer that is destined for you in Christ.

Victor D'Monte

ACKNOWLEDGEMENT

I take this opportunity to thank all those wonderful people who shaped my life during my journey of being a victorious Christian.

I am thankful to my wife, *Ann*, who has been with me for the last 30 years of my life, supporting and encouraging me in my journey with the Lord.

I would like to thank the Editor, *Ms. Esther S. Rajkumar*, for her valuable contribution in making this workbook a reality and for her patience and commitment in going through this material numerous times. I am also grateful to *Mr. Thomas Charles*, who helped with the design of this book and appreciate his dedication.

Victor D'Monte

FOREWORD

When one receives the Lord, it is such a joy to see the exuberance and happiness in the new believer. At first, their zeal often births a willingness to give up the most precious things of life and prioritize to know God. While hunger for the Kingdom is contagious, somewhere along the journey, their zeal and hunger are depleted, often resulting in them going back to living a nominal Christian life. I have wondered why there are so many malnourished and dwarf Christians. They were not meant to backslide, instead God meant for them to soar high like the eagles. Therefore, it is vital to understand what caused this decline, who is responsible for this, and most importantly, what should one do to overcome this trend.

In this book, the *'Keys to Victorious Living'*, *Ps. Victor D'Monte* deals with the antidote to prevent such erosion. Using the 'Armour of God' as a framework, he drives home the basic principles of discipleship and keys to live a victorious life as a conqueror, and not as a captive. He artfully covers the essential teachings such as understanding our part in the Spiritual Kingdom, importance of Church, knowing God, self and others, devotional life, fasting, establishing oneself in the Gospel of Peace, etc.. He clearly lays down the foundational teaching which can be used by every believer to become a disciple of the Lord Jesus Christ and to continue in the trajectory of growth in God. This book is designed for self-study and group study, with a combination of teaching, workbook, memory verse, and personal reflection. My favourite is the candid personal disclosure of *Ps. Victor D'Monte's* own life experiences in the section *"My Journal"*. His openness about his own learning in the early years of his walk with God will inspire anyone to keep trusting and growing in God.

I hope Churches, organizations, and individuals will adopt this book as a tool to teach and disciple believers, to help them be anchored on the foundations of the Word of God. I also hope that families will adopt this as a means to commence the discipleship process for their children in their homes.

Mr. Philips Dayanidhi
General Manager
(Corporate IT & Domain Digital)
BOSCH

HOW TO USE THIS WORKBOOK EFFECTIVELY

The two-fold objectives of this workbook are:
a. To enable you to walk in victory
b. To help you to disciple others by applying the truth you have learnt in this book

> II Timothy 2:2
> *"And the things that you have heard from me among many witnesses, commit these to faithful men who will be able to teach others also."*

For this workbook to be beneficial for you and to be an effective tool in your hands, you should follow the guidelines given below:

1. This study is recommended to be done in small groups of 4-5 people.
2. The leader of the group should facilitate discussion and encourage the participants to come up with their own answers.
3. Take time to **study** the Scriptures and fill in the appropriate blanks.
4. The Sword of the Holy Spirit is the Word of God. There is a 'MEMORY VERSE' section given at the end of each Lesson - it will be beneficial to memorise these verses.
5. Application is what makes a man wise. In each Lesson, there is a 'PERSONAL REFLECTION' section provided for you to write down how you will **apply** what you have learnt. The Bible says in I John 1:6, *"If we say that we have fellowship with Him, and walk in darkness, we lie and do not practice the truth"*.
6. Your determination (faith) and discipline to study and apply God's Word will help you to **grow** spiritually strong and achieve the goals mentioned at the end of each Lesson. The determination in your mind will make you self-dependent, but the determination in your spirit (faith) will make you God-dependent.

Determination (Faith) + Discipline = Growth

It is advisable for you not to take an academic approach to this, but to look at it as a means to enhance your walk with God and to establish you in victory.

INDEX

1.	A NEW BEGINNING	1
2.	THE BELT OF TRUTH	
	THE TRUTH ABOUT THE BIBLE AND GOD (PART I)	9
	BELIEF ABOUT YOURSELF AND OTHERS (PART II)	21
3.	THE BREASTPLATE OF RIGHTEOUSNESS	31
4.	THE GOSPEL OF PEACE	
	UNDERSTANDING OUR MISSION (PART I)	41
	ESTABLISHING YOURSELF IN THE GOSPEL (PART II)	49
5.	THE SHIELD OF FAITH	55
6.	THE HELMET OF SALVATION	63
7.	THE SWORD OF THE SPIRIT	71
8.	DEVOTIONAL LIFE	77
9.	KNOWING GOD'S WILL FOR YOUR LIFE	87
10.	WHY FASTING?	97
	ANSWERS	107
	EVALUATE YOUR PROGRESS	136

KEYS TO VICTORIOUS LIVING

LESSON I
A NEW BEGINNING

"For he has rescued us from the dominion (territory) *of darkness and brought us into the kingdom of the Son he loves ..." .* (Emphasis added)
- Colossians 1:13 (NIV)

Accepting Jesus as our Saviour is the beginning of a wonderful relationship with God. We begin this relationship with God knowing that He will never leave us nor forsake us. When you are born again, you become part of a new Kingdom and now belong to a spiritual family - the Church.

John 1:12-13 (NIV)
"Yet to all who did receive him, to those who believed in his name, he gave the right to become children of God (13) children born not of natural descent, nor of human decision or a husband's will, but born of God."

This Almighty God who created the universe became your Heavenly Father, the day you were born-again - you became His child, and the Church became your spiritual family.

The Church is the spiritual body of Christ that represents Jesus' Kingdom on Earth. This Kingdom is not a physical kingdom, but the **Rule of God on Earth through Jesus**, who came to reconcile man to God, setting us free from the bondage of sin and the Devil.

When Peter had a revelation of Jesus being the Son of God, Jesus said, *"I also say to you that you are Peter, and on this rock, I will build My church, and the gates of Hades shall not prevail against it"* (Matthew 16:18).

The Church is not a building, but a community of people who would be spiritually strong, that not even the gates of hell would prevail against them. Every building takes time to be built; in like manner, it takes time for us, His Church, to grow and become spiritually strong.

A good place to start is by recognising **Jesus as the only Door** to this spiritual Kingdom.
In John 10:9-10, Jesus says, *"I am the door. If anyone enters by Me, he will be saved and will go in*

and out and find pasture. (10) The thief does not come except to steal, and to kill, and to destroy. I have come that they may have life, and that they may have it more abundantly".

Jesus spoke of Himself as the only Door, indicating that there is only one way for us to be united with God - Jesus, the Lamb of God, is the only way for our sins to be forgiven.

Then in verse 10, Jesus exposes Satan's hidden identity as the thief who comes only to steal, kill and destroy. A thief is one who takes what does not belong to him and tries to get away without being caught. Jesus called the Devil a *"thief"* because his only agenda is to steal our joy, our peace with God, our health, our finances and above all our destiny, without us recognising that he (Satan) is the one behind our loss.

Today, many people battle with unresolved issues like addictions, anger, depression, sexual bondage, sickness and a lack of success, because they have not understood the spiritual reality behind these problems.

Satan has deceived many into thinking that God is the one who is responsible for all the chaos and suffering in this world, or that there is no God. This is a typical world view among most people. But, the Bible tells us in James 1:16-17, *"Do not be deceived, my beloved brethren. (17) _____ gift and _____ gift is from above, and comes down from the Father of lights, with whom there is no _____ or shadow of turning".*

On the other hand, Jesus made it clear that He is the Author of life, and the purpose of His coming into this world was to offer us life, and life more abundantly. In simple words, Jesus is the Giver of life - everything good comes from Him.

> What were these Christians in the above verse deceived about?
> They were deceived in their wrong understanding about God. James, an Apostle of Christ had to remind them that every good gift and every perfect gift comes from our Heavenly Father and He shows no partiality.

TWO KINGDOMS
When you accept Christ as your Lord and Saviour, you come under a new spiritual Kingdom.

Colossians 1:13 (NIV)
"For he has rescued us from the dominion (territory) *of darkness and brought us into the kingdom of the Son he loves ..."*. (Emphasis added)

The day you were born-again, you were transferred from the kingdom of darkness to the Kingdom of Light, and now God expects you to be governed by the principles of this new Kingdom. It is like a person who has migrated to another Country and is now left with no choice but to adapt to the culture of this Country.

In the Bible, the word 'Kingdom' refers to God's Kingly rule - His **Reign**, His **Action**, His **Lordship**, and His **Sovereign Governance**.

Jesus said to Nicodemus in John 3:3, *"Most assuredly, I say to you, unless one is born again, he cannot see the kingdom of God"*.

When God created mankind, He created us with the ability to live in both realms - the physical as well as the spiritual realm. It is only when we are born-again by the Spirit of God, will our spiritual eyes open to the reality of God's Word and the spiritual Kingdom of God.

In John 3:5, Jesus goes on to tell Nicodemus that, *"Most assuredly, I say to you, unless one is born of _____ and the _____, he cannot enter the kingdom of God"*.

The reference to the word *"water"*, is symbolic of the Word of God. For example, in Ephesians 5:26, the Bible says *"that He might sanctify and cleanse her* (Church) *with the washing of water by the word"* (Emphasis added).

> We can only enter into God's Kingdom by the work of the _____ and the _____.

Everything that God created since the beginning of this world came into existence through the Word and the Holy Spirit. Similarly, once we receive the Spirit of God, it is the Word of God that enables us to enter into this new Kingdom where we can experience His forgiveness, our deliverance, sanctification and healing. The Bible is God's Word to you and me where God instructs us on how we can live our lives in this new Kingdom.

Just as every other Earthly Kingdom is governed by a Government which sets the constitution for that Nation, the spiritual Kingdom of God is also governed by a Constitution that is laid down by Jesus Christ and established by the Church through the power of the Holy Spirit.

The meaning of 'Constitution' is *"the basic principles and laws of a nation, state, or social group that determine the powers and duties of the government and guarantee certain rights to the people in it"*.

THE CHURCH

We, the Church, are called to enforce this Constitution/Kingdom established by Jesus which Satan so fiercely opposes.

The Church is not made up of one man, but a group of people who stay committed to each other at all times. The Bible also encourages you to be part of one Church, where you relate with each other and support one another especially in times of difficulty.

> Ecclesiastes 12:11
> *"The words of the wise are like goads, and the words of scholars are like well-driven nails, given by **one** Shepherd."*

(A 'goad' is a stick that is used to drive cattle.)

The *"One Shepherd"* speaks of Jesus, and Pastors are under the One Shepherd who teaches people in-line with the Word of God (I Peter 5:2). The teaching of the Word of God should be like an instrument that guides you into the path of righteousness - and when you receive it, it will be like nails that are driven to hold you secure.

Today, many Christians are confused because they look to the internet, other resources (books, magazines, etc.) for their spiritual growth, instead of the teaching they receive from that one Shepherd whom God has placed over their lives. The Bible encourages us in Hebrews 10:25, *"Not forsaking the assembling of ourselves together, as is the manner of some, but exhorting one another, and so much the more as you see the Day approaching"*.

There are no lone rangers in God's Kingdom. Just as a piece of coal needs to be in contact with other burning coals to keep the fire burning, every one of us also need to be in contact with other Christians, to stay on the path that we have chosen.

Every new born baby needs to be fed and nurtured by his/her family; in the same way, every new Christian needs to be fed and nurtured spiritually, and be a part of a spiritual family, who will help shape them into the person God intended them to be.

A burning coal, as hot as it may be, cannot remain on fire if it is alone. It must have heat and protection from the other coals in the fire. Left alone, it would become cold. In like manner, no Christian, as firm as his decision for Christ may be, can be victorious without the help and encouragement of other believers. We need one another, to remain faithful to God in the midst of trials, difficulties and opposition. It is so easy to take Church life for granted, yet it is a very vital part for our spiritual growth.

Some people think they need to become Holy before qualifying to go to Church. This is a mistake. There are also some who go to Church, but believe that if they sin then they should no longer attend. The Church itself works to mature you. The truth is, not even the admired leaders have walked perfectly and without stumbling since they gave their lives to the Lord. They are today in this position of honour because they learned how to confess their mistakes to God immediately, and continued faithfully in the Church, despite the errors they made.

Remember, the Church that Jesus built was meant for sinners and not just for Saints. So, even if you make a mistake and feel ashamed, confess your sin to God, and do not miss Church. Your commitment to the Church will actually uphold and lift you up to new levels of victory. Remember, being a part of a Church should not be a matter of convenience; it should be a spiritual decision, knowing that God placed you there for your spiritual growth.

> Which local Church are you a part of?
>
> _____

If you haven't made the decision, ask the Lord to guide you to the right fellowship.

CHOOSING THE RIGHT CHURCH

The four things that you need to look at while making your decision to be a part of a Church are as follows:
- Is the doctrine of the Church in line with the Bible?
- Do you agree with the vision of the Church?
- Is it a place of belonging and freedom?
- Does it have a lake mentality or a river mentality?

> (A lake mentality is when a Pastor only focuses on the Church growing numerically, whereas, a river mentality is when a Church is committed to seeing people grow from being baby Christians to mature Christians fulfilling their spiritual gifts, calling, destiny.)

And when you become a part of a Church, determine in your heart not to just occupy a seat in Church, but rather, give it the best of your time, commitment and service. As you do this, you will soon begin to see your love for your Church and for other believers grow.

It is important to know that even as you do this, there are two things that you require in order to grow in any area of your life:
- Determination (Faith)
- Discipline

When our determination comes out of our will, it can lead to self-effort, but when it comes from our spirit, it stems from 'Faith in Jesus', and this kind of determination is what transforms us.

For example, if you want to grow physically strong, you need to have the determination and discipline to exercise regularly. Similarly, if you want to grow spiritually strong, it will require your determination and discipline to grow in the understanding and application of the Word of God.

Living the Christian life gives you a new beginning, a fresh start to live life. It changes the way you relate to God and one another, but more importantly, it gives you a new purpose for living.

PERSONAL REFLECTION

Why are you a part of your Church?

_____

_____

_____

_____

MEMRY VERSE

"For he has rescued us from the dominion (territory) of darkness and brought us into the kingdom of the Son he loves …".

Colossians 1:13 (NIV)

GAL

Be committed to a local Church, where you can grow and serve in a meaningful way.

REVIEW OF LESSON I

Which are the two spiritual Kingdoms?
_____
_____

What are the two things that you need to be consistent with, in order to grow in any aspect of your life?
_____
_____

How did you apply Lesson I in your life?
_____
_____

Write down the memory verse you learnt last week?
_____
_____

Determination (Faith) + Discipline = Growth

LESSON II
THE BELT OF TRUTH

PART I
THE TRUTH ABOUT THE BIBLE AND GOD

"Therefore take up the whole armour of God, that you may be able to withstand in the evil day, and having done all, to stand.".
- Ephesians 6:13

We need to put on the 'whole' Armour of God, in order for us to be victorious. God gave us this spiritual Armour so that we could withstand the works of the enemy. This Armour is the Truth concerning the work of God in the various significant areas of our lives.

So, let us now begin our study by looking at the different pieces of the Armour that God has given us.

The first piece of the Armour is mentioned in Ephesians 6:14 - *"Stand, therefore, having girded your waist with _____ ..."*.

Truth is more than just the verses in the Bible - **Truth is a Person, and this Person is Jesus.**

In John 14:6, Jesus said to them, *"I am the way, the **truth**, and the life. No one comes to the Father except through Me"*.

The Bible is the inspired Word of God and it gives you a revelation of God, His infinite character, His infinite power and His promises concerning you. Therefore, one must not read the Bible just to know what is written in it; but, one should read the Bible to know God.

John 8:31-32
"To the Jews who had believed him, Jesus said, 'If you hold to my teaching, you are really my disciples. (32) Then you will know the truth, and the truth will set you free'."

Truth is essential because truth does not change based on circumstances. Truth can be your best friend if you embrace it, but if you resist it, it could be your worst enemy. Truth is constant; so, when you build your life on truth, your life will be more secure.

Truth is not based on what you feel; it is not subjective. I am sure you will agree with me when I say that our emotions are unreliable, because they can change any minute. One negative/positive word or thought can change the way you feel the entire day.

Let us now look at four essential and unchangeable truths that you will be able to count on at all times.

1. THE TRUTH CONCERNING THE BIBLE

The Bible is the infallible Word of God. It is divided into two sections - the Old Testament and the New Testament. It consist of 39 books in the Old Testament and 27 in the New Testament.

> The Old Testament consists of the books of Law (5) + History (12) + Poetry (5) + Major Prophets (5) + Minor Prophets (12).
>
> The New Testament consists of The Gospels (4) + History (1) + Letters to the Church (21) + Prophecy (1).

The word 'Testament' originally meant 'covenant', 'agreement' or 'will'. The Old Testament records God's original covenant or agreement with humanity, and the New Testament records the new covenant that God made through His Son, Jesus Christ. These two agreements are about restoring sinful man to a right relationship with God. And please know that the God of the Old Testament is the God of the New Testament - the only difference is the **remedy for sin**.

Under God's agreement in the Old Testament, blood sacrifices of animals were made by man to obtain forgiveness of sin. It is interesting to note that these sacrifices in the Old Testament were actually symbolic of Jesus' ultimate sacrifice in the New Testament, which was provided under the new agreement with God. This final sacrifice for sin was made through the birth, life, death, and resurrection of Jesus. Jesus sacrificed His own life so that you and I, even as we find ourself in our sinful state, can come before a Holy God with confidence.

> **Write down the names of all the books in the New Testament under each section:**
>
> The Gospels:
> _____
>
> Books of History:
> _____
>
> Letters to the Church:
> _____
> _____
>
> Prophecy:
> _____

The Bible is united in its contents
The Bible is one book, but is written by at least 40 different people, many of whom never saw each other, and it was written over a period of around 1,500 years. Yet, the **unity** and **continuity** in its contents are so apparent that it is easy for us to think that there was just one author - and that is none other than God Himself.

> II Timothy 3:16 (ESV)
> *"All Scripture is breathed out by God and profitable for teaching, for reproof, for correction, and for training in righteousness."*

Even though the Bible was written over many years, there are no contradictions. One writer does not contradict any of the others. They all spoke on various subjects with much harmony, starting from the first book of Genesis, right up to the last book of Revelation. This was only possible because there is only **one Author - The Holy Spirit.** All the writers wrote the Bible under the direction and inspiration of the Holy Spirit, and this is why the Bible does not contradict itself.

> Matthew 24:35
> *"Jesus said that Heaven and Earth will pass away but His Word* (Truth) *will not pass away."* (Emphasis added)

2. YOUR BELIEF ABOUT GOD

Exodus 34:6 (NIV)
"And he passed in front of Moses, proclaiming, 'The Lord, the Lord, the compassionate and gracious God, slow to anger, abounding in love (steadfast love (ESV)) *and faithfulness'."*
(Emphasis added)

These five characteristics of God (mentioned in the above verse) give us a clear understanding of who God is. **His character and nature should lay the foundation for our faith in God. Jesus is everything the Father is.**

John 1:1-4, 14
"In the beginning was the Word, and the Word was with God, and the Word was God. (2) He was with God in the beginning. (3) Through him all things were made; without him nothing was made that has been made. (4) In him was life, and that life was the light of all mankind."

(14) "The Word became flesh and made his dwelling among us. We have seen his glory, the glory of the one and only Son, who came from the Father, full of grace and truth."

- God is Compassionate/Merciful
These two words are interchangeable in the Bible, depending on which translation you use. We are all guilty of breaking God's Law according to God's standard of Holiness, and the consequences of this is punishment. But, God extends His mercy towards us. Mercy is about not getting what we deserve (i.e. punishment for all our wickedness and rebellion against Him). God is a just God, but He chose to demonstrate His mercy towards us by granting us forgiveness in the place of punishment.

Psalm 103:10-12
"He has not dealt with us according to our sins, nor punished us according to our iniquities. (11) For as the heavens are high above the earth, so great is His mercy toward those who fear Him; (12) as far as the east is from the west, so far has He removed our transgressions from us."

Read the following Scriptures and write down these verses regarding God's Compassion/Mercy towards you.

Psalm 51:1 (NIV)
"Have mercy on me, O God, according to your unfailing love; according to your great compassion blot out my transgressions."

Psalm 119:77

_____
_____

Isaiah 49:10 (NIV)

_____
_____

Isaiah 49:13 (NIV)
"Shout for joy, you heavens; rejoice, you earth; burst into song, you mountains! For the Lord comforts his people and will have compassion on his afflicted ones."

- God is Gracious

The word 'Grace' is like two sides of a coin.

The first meaning of the word 'Grace' is God's unmerited favour. This meaning demonstrates that God's acceptance towards you is not based on how good you are, but on how gracious He is.

The acronym for GRACE is:

G - Great
R - Riches
A - At
C - Christ's
E - Expense

The second meaning for 'Grace' is God's Divine Ability. This meaning demonstrates God's ability to transform you into the Image He created you.

Genesis 1:27
"So God created man in His own image; in the image of God He created him; male and female He created them."

Read the following Scriptures and write down these verses regarding our God who is Gracious.

Joel 2:13
"So rend your heart, and not your garments; return to the Lord your God, for He is gracious and merciful, slow to anger, and of great kindness; and He relents from doing harm."

John 1:17

_____

_____

Titus 2:11
"For the grace of God that brings salvation has appeared to all men…".

Isaiah 30:18 (NIV)

_____

_____

- God is slow to anger

Anger is an emotion that God expresses towards injustice, and He gets angry when we deliberately walk in sin. It is important to remember that **God loves the sinner but hates the sin**. He hates sin because sin robs us from walking in His Blessing, and tarnishes the Image in which He created us.

Jesus bore the anger and justice of God that we rightfully deserved for all ours sins when He died on the cross. In this way, Jesus met the demands for justice; had He not done this, you and I would not be in a position to receive His mercy.

Read the following Scriptures and write down these verses regarding God's anger.

Psalm 145:8
"The Lord is gracious and full of compassion, slow to anger and great in mercy."

Jonah 4:2b

_____

_____

Nahum 1:3a

_____

_____

- God abounds in Love
The one word that describes God is *'Love'* (I John 4:8). The Bible defines Love in I Corinthians 13:4-5:

> Love suffers long.
> Love is kind.
> Love does not envy.
> Love does not boast.
> Love is not proud.
> Love does not dishonour others.
> Love is not self-seeking.
> Love is not easily angered.
> Love keeps no record of wrongs.

All of the above characteristics describe the nature of God towards us. Jesus was the manifestation of God on Earth, and Jesus expressed the above qualities of God through His life and Ministry.

Lamentations 3:22-23 (ESV)
"The steadfast love of the Lord never ceases; His mercies never come to an end; (23) they are new every morning; great is your faithfulness."

The *"steadfast love of the Lord"* signifies that God's Love does not waver. In other words, there is nothing that you could ever do to get God to love you more, nor is there anything you can do that will cause God to love you any less. His Love is constant. You and I are recipients of His Love because of who He is.

> **Read the following Scriptures and write down these verses regarding God's abounding Love for you.**
>
> Psalm 36:7
> *"How precious is Your lovingkindness, O God! Therefore the children of men put their trust under the shadow of Your wings."*
>
> Romans 8:38-39
> *"For I am persuaded that neither death nor life, nor angels nor principalities nor powers, nor things present nor things to come, (39) _____*
> *_____*
> *_____*
>
> Romans 5:8
> *"But God demonstrates His own love toward us, in that while we were still sinners, Christ died for us."*
>
> Romans 8:32
> _____
> _____

- God is Faithful

You can depend on God, because He is Faithful, and enter His presence with boldness and confidence because of what Jesus has done for you.

Hebrews 10:19
"Therefore, brethren, having boldness to enter the Holiest by the blood of Jesus, (20) by a new and living way which He consecrated for us, through the veil, that is, His flesh…".

> **Read the following Scriptures and write down these verses regarding God's Faithfulness.**
>
> Psalm 36:5
> *"Your mercy, O Lord, is in the heavens; Your faithfulness reaches to the clouds."*

Psalm 40:11 (NIV)

_____

_____

Hebrews 10:23
"Let us hold fast the confession of our hope without wavering, for He who promised is faithful."

II Timothy 2:13 (ISV)
"Our faith may fail, his never wanes—That's who he is, he cannot change!"

I Thessalonians 5:24

_____

_____

It is easier to have faith to trust the Promises of God when you know the Character of God.

> Worship is acknowledging God for who He is. Take a few minutes to just worship God and thank Him for who He is. You can make this your daily practice; this will help you to experience the attributes of God, which you have just learnt about.

MY JOURNAL

"Like many others, I also tried to fit God into my world, and was disillusioned about Him when I saw the hatred, suffering, poverty and violence all around; I wondered why God was not doing anything about it. And this lack of understanding about God led me to become an atheist.

But today as I look back, I have realised that in our finite minds, we try and fit the Almighty God into our understanding, but God sent His Son Jesus into our world so that through Him, He could draw us into His World. Many of us have allowed our circumstances to shape our beliefs about God. But it is important that we allow our beliefs about God, to shape our beliefs concerning our circumstances. It is this truth about God that has enabled me to overcome the most difficult and challenging circumstances, over the years, in my life."

PERSONAL REFLECTION

Write down three things that impressed you the most from this Lesson regarding the Bible and God.

THE BIBLE:

_____
_____
_____

GOD:

_____
_____
_____

MEMRY VERSE

" … *and be renewed in the spirit of your mind, (24) and that you put on the new man which was created according to God, in true righteousness and holiness".*

Ephesians 4:23-24

Belt of Truth

GOAL

To align your beliefs with God's Word.

REVIEW OF LESSON II (PART I)

What are the five Characteristics of God that you have learnt in this lesson, and which is the one that ministered to you?

1. _____
2. _____
3. _____
4. _____
5. _____

How did you apply Lesson II (Part I) in your life?
_____
_____

Write down the memory verse you learnt last week?
_____
_____

Determination (Faith) + Discipline = Growth

LESSON II
THE BELT OF TRUTH

PART II
BELIEF ABOUT YOURSELF AND OTHERS

"So God created man in His own image; in the image of God He created him; male and female He created them."
- Genesis 1:27

If you have a wrong view about God, then there could be chances that you may have a wrong belief about yourself and also about others. In Romans 1:18, the Bible tells us that when people who were godless suppressed the truth by their wickedness, He gave them up to their futile and foolish hearts. Therefore, God gave them over to their shameful lusts, and their belief about themselves and others were distorted (Verse 26).

In this lesson, as we look at the Scriptures, you will discover the truth about yourself and about others.

1. YOUR BELIEF ABOUT YOURSELF

Our identity is relational. You were born with a natural identity which came from your parents. This identity shaped the way you think about yourself and others. What your parents said about you, both positive as well as negative, has had a considerable influence over your life.

The question, *"Who am I?"*, is a mystery to many. As a result, people strive to develop their identity from their status, work, achievements, etc.. But, you were born into a relationship with God when you were born-again. Once you recognise God as your Heavenly Father, your identity will no longer be in what you do (achievements, etc.), but in who you are.

When Jesus came into this world, He came to reveal who God is. And as a perfect human-being, He also came to reveal our true identity in God. **God sent Jesus as the prototype to show us how**

He intended mankind to be.

Your spiritual identity is your true identity.

You must believe that God created you for greatness, and not for failure. When God created you, He had a purpose for you.

> Take a moment now, and comprehend the truth that God created you to be just like Him! :) You were created to think the way God thinks, to have His emotions of love, kindness, self-control, anger, etc..

Here are some truths that will help you re-discover your true identity in Christ:

If God said that you are **justified** in Christ, then you are.
If God said that you are **forgiven**, then you are.
If God said that you are **loved unconditionally**, then you are.
If God said that you are **accepted wholeheartedly**, then you are.
If God said that you are **more than a conqueror**, then you are.
If God said that you are a **Child of God**, and He is your Heavenly Father, then that is what you need to believe.

God no longer looks at you as a sinner, but as righteous because you are in Christ. And the way you put on the new identity is by constantly renewing your mind knowing who you are in Christ.

> Romans 3:4
> *"...Indeed, let God be true but every man a liar. As it is written: 'That You may be justified in Your words, and may overcome when You are judged'"*.

> Ephesians 4:23-24 (NIV)
> *"...to be made _____ in the attitude of your minds; (24) and to put on the _____ (identity), created to be like God in true righteousness and holiness"*. (Emphasis added)

You will never discover your destiny if you do not discover your true identity. For example, Jacob, whose name means 'deceiver', had an encounter with God, which resulted in God changing his name to 'Israel', which means 'Prince with God'. Notice that God first changed his identity before He changed his destiny. And there are many more examples in the Bible to illustrate this truth.

> **MY JOURNAL**
>
> *"I must confess, I too grew up like most people in a very negative environment. I constantly heard negative words spoken about me. And the worst part was that I believed those negative words and allowed them to influence me. That caused me to look at my life and circumstances through the eyes of rejection and failure. Until one day, I discovered that the truth concerning my identity was not in what others (parents, friends, etc.) said about me, but is in what God says about me."*

We must not only discover the truth about who God is, but we must also have a revelation concerning the truth about who we are in God. The people of Israel had the right belief about God, but they also had a wrong understanding of who they were in God, which ultimately deprived them of the Promise Land.

You will go on to live a victorious life when you have a Biblical view of both - who God is and who you are.

If you are finding it difficult to accept yourself because of a wrong identity, it would be good for you to share this with the person who is discipling you.

4. YOUR BELIEF ABOUT OTHERS

When God created mankind, He created us all in the Image of God, irrespective of our caste, creed or colour. We must have a paradigm shift in our minds, to view every human being as those who God created in His own Image and likeness.

Most of us have grown up in an environment where it is common to undermine and ridicule people for who they are and for what they do. Very few people cultivate a positive attitude of respect towards others.

We are all made in the Image of God.

> James 3:8-10 (NIV)
> *"But no human being can tame the tongue. It is a restless evil, full of deadly poison. (9) With the tongue, we praise our Lord and Father, and with it, we curse human beings, who have been made in God's likeness. (10) Out of the same mouth come praise and cursing. My brothers and sisters, this should not be."*

In the following verse, underline the attitude that we must have towards one another

Romans 15:7 (NIV)
"Accept one another, then, just as Christ accepted you, in order to bring praise to God."

In the following verses, write down your responsibility towards one another:

Colossians 3:13
"Bearing with one another, and forgiving one another, if anyone has a complaint against another; even as Christ forgave you, so you also must do."

_____

Mark 11:25
"And whenever you stand praying, if you have anything against anyone, forgive him, that your Father in heaven may also forgive you your trespasses."

_____

Read James 2:1-3, and write down the one thing that we should not do with regards to those who are poor?

_____

In today's context, how would you apply what Galatians 3:28 says?

_____

_____

OUR GOD-GIVEN RESPONSIBILITY TOWARDS GOD AND OTHERS

Most of our obedience towards God is worked out in our relationships with others.

In the ten commandments, only the first two commandments are towards God; the remaining eight are concerning our responsibility towards one another.

The first two commands towards God are:

Exodus 20:3-4
"You shall _____ before Me. (4) "You shall _____ any likeness of anything that is in heaven above, or that is in the earth beneath, or that is in the water under the earth ...".

Exodus 20:7
"You shall not take _____, for the Lord will not hold him guiltless who takes His name in vain."

The next eight commandments are with regards to one another:

Exodus 20:8-10
"'Remember _____, to keep it holy.' (9) Six days you shall labor and do all your work, (10) but the seventh day is the Sabbath of the Lord your God. In it you shall do no work: you, nor your son, nor your daughter, nor your male servant, nor your female servant, nor your cattle, nor your stranger who is within your gates."

Exodus 20:12
"_____, that your days may be long upon the land which the Lord your God is giving you."

Read Ephesians 6:2-3 and write down the two blessings you receive when you honour your father and mother.

1. _____

2. _____

Remember, honour has to do with respect, and not obedience.

Exodus 20:13
"You shall not _____."

I John 3:15
"Whoever hates his brother is a murderer, and you know that no murderer has eternal life abiding in him."

Exodus 20:14
"You shall not commit _____."

Matthew 5:28-29
"But I say to you that whoever looks at a woman to lust for her has already committed adultery with her in his heart. (29) If your right eye causes you to sin, pluck it out and cast it from you; for it is more profitable for you that one of your members perish, than for your whole body to be cast into hell."

Hebrews 13:4
"Marriage is honourable among all, and the bed undefiled; but fornicators and adulterers God will judge."

Exodus 20:15
"You shall not _____."

Ephesians 4:28
"Let him who stole steal no longer, but rather let him labor, working with his hands what is good, that he may have something to give him who has need."

Exodus 20:16
"You shall not _____ against your neighbour."

Ephesians 4:25
"Therefore, putting away lying, 'Let each one of you speak truth with his neighbour,' for we are members of one another."

Exodus 20:17
"You shall _____ your neighbour's house; you shall not covet your neighbour's wife, nor his male servant, nor his female servant, nor his ox, nor his donkey, nor anything that is your neighbour's."

I Corinthians 5:11
"But now I have written to you not to keep company with anyone named a brother, who is sexually immoral, or covetous, or an idolater, or a reviler, or a drunkard, or an extortioner— not even to eat with such a person."

How does the New Testament sum up all the ten commandments in Romans 13:9?

_____

_____

Obeying this list of what God has commanded us may seem beyond our ability, but in reality, when we love God and we love one another, we automatically fulfil the ten commandments. It is for this reason that **Jesus gave us only two commandments to keep - to love God, and to love one another**.

Matthew 22:37-40
"Jesus said to him, "'You shall love the Lord your God with all your heart, with all your soul, and with all your mind.' (38) This is the first and great commandment. (39) And the second is like it: 'You shall love your neighbour as yourself.' (40) On these two commandments hang all the Law and the Prophets."

When you gird your mind with this Truth, it helps you:
- To have a right relationship with God
- To have a Godly perspective of ourselves
- To have a healthy attitude towards others

> When a soldier prepares for battle, he never forgets to strap on his belt because his belt fulfils the very crucial function of keeping his sword, dagger and tunic attached. In the same way, it is the Belt of Truth - God's Word (who God is, who we are in God, and how we view others), which holds every piece of the Armour together and this protects us in battle.

PERSONAL REFLECTION

There is a difference between the truth and a feeling. Our feelings may vary according to our surroundings and circumstances; they change from time-to-time, but, the truth is permanent. For example, 2+2=4 is the truth and does not change, whereas, our feelings can change according to our emotions.

The truth of God's Word is eternal and not subject to circumstances. Jesus said in Matthew 24:35, *"Heaven and earth will pass away, but My words will by no means pass away"* - this is the eternal truth.

Write down one truth that you learnt in Lesson II which has made a big impact on you.

_____

_____

PERSONAL REFLECTION

Your relationship with people is just as important as your relationship with God. Write down the three things that impressed you the most from this Lesson, regarding yourself and others.

YOURSELF:

_____
_____
_____

OTHERS:

_____
_____
_____

Do you have a positive attitude towards other people?

MEM🧠RY VERSE

"And he passed in front of Moses, proclaiming, 'The Lord, the Lord, the compassionate and gracious God, slow to anger, abounding in love and faithfulness.'"

Exodus 34:6 (NIV)

Belt of Truth

G🎯AL

To grow in your knowledge and experience of God.

REVIEW OF LESSON II (PART II)

God no longer looks at you as a sinner, but as _____ because you are in Christ.

Your _____ identity is your true identity.

Most of our obedience towards God is worked out in our _____ with others.

What are the two commandments that Jesus gave us to keep?
_____
_____

How did you apply Lesson II (Part II) in your life?
_____
_____

Write down the memory verse you learnt last week?
_____
_____

Determination (Faith) + Discipline = Growth

LESSON III

THE BREASTPLATE OF RIGHTEOUSNESS

"For He made Him who knew no sin to be sin for us, that we might become the righteousness of God in Him.".
- II Corinthians 5:21

Jesus became our sin offering so that we would be declared righteous before God. This righteousness is a gift that gives us the ability to stand before God with confidence. Apart from Christ, we can never achieve a right standing before God. We don't sin and then become sinners; we are born as sinners and are therefore prone to sin. It is for this reason that we find doing the wrong thing seems much easier than doing what is right.

We have all cultivated an inborn tendency to base our righteousness on what we do. We come from different cultural and religious backgrounds, and this also adds to our tendency. Religion teaches people to follow certain rituals, so that one can gain merit/favour before their God.

> According to the Bible 'sin' is 'falling short of God's mark (standard) of Holiness'. Therefore, it is for this reason that we cannot attain God's standard of righteousness in our effort.

Sin is not the presence of evil, but the absence of God's Holiness.

Religion teaches us to put our faith in sacrifices and self-effort to please God. Whereas, Christianity is about a Holy God reaching out to sinful man. Christianity is about putting our faith in Christ and His finished work for us on the cross.

In every religion, there are certain rituals and practices (for example, chanting mantras, the rosary, reciting prayers in a ritualistic manner, etc.) that need to be adhered to for God to hear their prayers. But, Jesus said in Matthew 6:7, *"When you pray, do not use vain repetitions as the heathen do. For they think that they will be heard for their many words".*

Hebrews 10:10
" ... *we have been sanctified through the offering of the body of Jesus Christ _____".*

Religion began in the heart of man, whereas Christianity originated in the Heart of God. The Bible says in John 3:16, *"For God so loved the world that He gave His only begotten Son, that whoever believes in Him should not perish but have everlasting life".*

THERE ARE TWO KINDS OF RIGHTEOUSNESS

The first kind of righteousness is derived by following specific rules and laws in a ritualistic manner. The Pharisees are a good example of this form of spirituality in the New Testament. 'Pharisees' were a sect in the Jewish community who strictly adhered to following the ceremonial laws of that time. This righteousness is based on our self-effort to be right with God.

Righteousness based on self-effort will always lead to legalism and ultimately results in self-righteousness and pride.

Isaiah 64:6
"But we are all like an unclean thing, and all our righteousnesses are like filthy rags ...".

The second kind of righteousness is a **righteousness that comes by faith**.

Romans 10:4
"For Christ is the end of the law for righteousness to everyone who believes."

Romans 3:21-22
"But now the righteousness of God apart from the law is revealed, being witnessed by the Law and the Prophets, (22) even the righteousness of God, through faith in Jesus Christ, to all and on all who believe ...".

We must be careful not to make Christianity another religion by putting our faith in our own righteousness to please God. **Our salvation and forgiveness of sins are received only by faith in Jesus' sacrifice on the cross.**

Christianity is about putting our faith in Jesus' ability not only to forgive us, but to also cleanse us from all our unrighteousness, to deliver us, and to heal us. Once we come to Christ, we must give up our self-dependence, and start living our lives depending on Him (faith).

Romans 10:3
"For they being ignorant of God's righteousness, and seeking to establish their own righteousness, have not submitted to the righteousness of God."

We attain the righteousness of God by first believing in our heart (spirit) and then confessing with our mouth what Jesus accomplished for us on the cross.

Romans 10:9-10
"If you confess with your mouth the Lord Jesus and believe in your heart that God has raised Him from the dead, you will be saved. (10) For with the heart one believes unto righteousness, and with the mouth confession is made unto salvation".

> Believing is with the _____ and confession is with the _____.

In the verse given below, underline what stands out as the most important aspect for you.

Romans 11:6
"And if by grace, then it is no longer of works; otherwise grace is no longer grace. But if it is of works, it is no longer grace; otherwise work is no longer work".

Colossians 1:21-22
"And you, who once were alienated and enemies in your mind by wicked works, yet now He has reconciled (22) in the body of His flesh through death, to present you holy, and blameless, and above reproach in His sight …".

The word 'righteousness' means 'right-standing before God'. And it is this right-standing before God that gives us the confidence to come boldly to the Throne of Grace. But for the righteousness of God, we would all have stood condemned before Him. This righteousness is God's gift (grace) to us.

Hebrews 4:16
"Let us therefore come boldly to the throne of grace, that we may obtain mercy and find grace to help in time of need".

No one is perfect, not even your most admired Leader or Pastor. So, when you fall short in some way or the other, you must learn to come before God based on His righteousness, to receive the forgiveness of sins and cleansing from all unrighteousness.

In I John 1:9, the Bible says, *"If we confess our sins, He is faithful and just to forgive us our sins and to cleanse us from all unrighteousness".*

'Confession' is not about you telling God what you did, because He already knows what you did; confession is about you 'agreeing with God that what you did was wrong'.

When we confess our sin before God, He is, _____ and __ _____ to _____ us our sins and to _____ us from all unrighteousness.

> **What do I confess with my mouth?**
> _____
> _____
>
> **What do I do with my heart?**
> _____
> _____

We become free of the guilt of what we have done when we receive God's forgiveness. We must learn to _____ His forgiveness by _____. And we must learn to forgive ourselves and move on.

In the second part of the above verse, the Bible says that God is faithful and just to _____ us from all unrighteousness. The dictionary meaning for the word 'cleanse' is to make 'something, (especially the skin) thoroughly clean'. This is what God does when we receive His forgiveness by faith. He makes our spirit thoroughly clean - no guilt, no condemnation. And this is what enables us to come boldly to the Throne of Grace, where we can obtain mercy. God's Throne is not a throne of judgement, but a Throne of Grace.

> **Isaiah 43:25**
> _____
> _____

Even as we come before God in boldness, we must trust Him for His grace, to overcome sin in our life.

It is important to know that there is a difference between having a relationship with God and your fellowship with God. The best way to explain this is through an example - when you disobey your parents and deliberately do wrong, your fellowship with your parents is affected, but your relationship with them as their child never changes. In like manner, every time we sin, it is our fellowship with God that is affected, and not our relationship.

Galatians 4:5-7
"But when the fullness of the time had come, God sent forth His Son, born of a woman, born under the law, (6) And because you are sons, God has sent forth the Spirit of His Son into your hearts, crying out, 'Abba, Father!' (7) Therefore you are no longer a slave but a son, and if a son, then an heir of God through Christ."

Galatians 3:26
"For you are all sons of God through faith in Christ Jesus."

Difference between a slave and a son
Sons have a sense of **belonging**, whereas, slaves do not.
Sons know they are **accepted**; slaves need to earn their acceptance.
Sons are **entitled to an inheritance**, but slaves are not.
A slave can stop being a slave (servant) whenever his master wants … but, a son does not stop being a son.

When you have lost your free-will to choose, it is bondage. Bondage is about you handing over your free-will to some substance (drugs, etc.) or activity (sex, video-games, etc.), to the extent that you are unable to stop even when you want to do so. All forms of addiction make us slaves and rob us of our freedom.

The gift of righteousness must result in you living a righteous life in the power of the Holy Spirit. When a Christian is still in bondage to sin despite of being disciplined in prayer, fasting and meditating on God's Word, then James 5:16 is a helpful solution.

James 5:16
*"**Confess your trespasses** (sin) to one another, and pray for one another, that you may be healed. The effective, fervent prayer of a righteous man avails much."* (Emphasis added)

It is for your healing and deliverance that the Bible instructs you to confess your sin to one another (someone who is spiritually mature, preferably your Pastor/leader or ministry team person). And even as you receive prayer for this specific area of your life, trust God for His intervention.

As explained earlier, our righteousness is established out of our relationship with Christ. Jesus gives us a very graphic picture in John 15, of how our relationship with Him should be.

John 15:4-5
"Abide in Me, and I in you. As the branch cannot bear fruit of itself, unless it abides in the vine, neither can you, unless you abide in Me. (5) 'I am the vine, you are the branches. He who abides in Me, and I in him, bears much fruit; for without Me you can do nothing'."

The Bible clearly says that Jesus is The Vine and we are the branches. Because we are all descendants of Adam, we were all once rooted 'in Adam'; as a result, deceit, lying, anger, etc., came naturally to us.

But now, having accepted Christ, you are broken-off from Adam, and grafted into The Vine who is Jesus Christ.

> Romans 5:18-19 (ESV)
> *"Therefore, as one trespass led to condemnation for all men, so one act of righteousness leads to justification and life for all men. (19) For as by the one man's* (Adam) *disobedience many were made sinners, so by the one man's* (Jesus Christ) *obedience the many will be made righteous."* (Emphasis added)

A branch cannot bear fruit by itself unless it is attached to the tree. So, once you have accepted Jesus as your Saviour, you are then grafted into Christ, with a new identity and belonging. Therefore, God has grafted you as a branch into The Vine (Jesus), so that you would manifest the fruit of The Vine. Christians are an extension of the character and power of Christ that is expressed through us.

Why should you abide in The Vine?

_____

_____

The Christian life is about Christ living His life through us.

We are called 'Christ-ians' because we are disciples of Christ, called to live a transformed life in the power of Christ.

The Bible says in Colossians 1:21-23, *"And you, who once were alienated and enemies in your mind by wicked works, yet now He has reconciled (22) in the body of His flesh through death, to present you holy, and blameless, and above reproach in His sight. (23) if indeed you continue in the faith, grounded and steadfast, and are not moved away from the hope of the gospel which you heard ..."*.

The basis for which God answers our prayer is not based on our righteousness, but on His righteousness.

> II Corinthians 1:20
> *"For all the promises of God _____ (Christ) _____, and _____, to the glory of God through us."* (Emphasis added)

MY JOURNAL

"As a new Christian, I found it a challenge to believe God to answer my prayers. I struggled to trust God for my life and the circumstances I found myself in. Every time I prayed, I had condemning thoughts of how unworthy I was to stand before a Holy God. These thoughts made me think that God would never answer my prayers because I failed to live up to His standards. This was an on going battle until one day, God gave me a revelation from His Word in II Corinthians 1:20, "For all the promises of God in Him are Yes, and in Him Amen, to the glory of God through us". It was only then that it dawned on me - that all the promises of God are "Yes" in Christ's righteousness, and not in my righteousness. From that day on, my faith and worship grew as I focused on this amazing gift of righteousness which God has given us - to stand with boldness and confidence in His presence."

The promises of God are not only *"Yes in Christ"* but, they are also *"Amen in Christ"*. The word 'Amen' means 'so be it'. So, when God answers our prayers, it is for His glory - we cannot take credit for it. When we arm ourselves with God's righteousness, it gives us the confidence to pray, believing God to hear our prayers.

When you are girded with the Breastplate of Righteousness, it secures your standing before God - free from guilt and condemnation. It also gives you the confidence, knowing that God will answer your prayers.

Just as a physical breastplate protects the soldier's heart, it is the Breastplate of Righteousness that protects your spirit (heart) from guilt and condemnation.

PERSONAL REFLECTION

Write down what you have learnt from this lesson regarding how God sees you, before you came to Christ and after you received Christ.

_____
_____
_____

Do you still struggle with thoughts of guilt and condemnation?

MEM🧠RY VERSE

"For the eyes of the Lord are on the righteous, and His ears are open to their prayers; but the face of the Lord is against those who do evil."

I Peter 3:12

G🎯AL

Enjoy God's promises that He has given you, based on His righteousness.

REVIEW OF LESSON III

Sin is not the presence of evil, but the _____.

Write down what are the two kinds of righteousness that the Bible talks about?

1. _____

2. _____

How do you receive your forgiveness?
_____

The basis for which God answers our prayer is not based on our righteousness, but _____ _____.

How did you apply Lesson III in your life?
_____
_____

Write down the memory verse you learnt last week?
_____
_____

Determination (Faith) + Discipline = Growth

LESSON IV
THE GOSPEL OF PEACE

PART I
UNDERSTANDING OUR MISSION

*"And the God of peace will crush Satan under your feet shortly.
The grace of our Lord Jesus Christ be with you. Amen."*
- Romans 16:20

Ephesians 6:15
"... and having shod your feet with the preparation of the gospel of peace."

GOD'S COMPASSION

In Luke 2, God sent a whole host of Angels to communicate His Will to us.

Luke 2:13-14
"And suddenly there was with the angel a multitude of the heavenly host praising God and saying: (14) 'Glory to God in the highest, and on earth peace, goodwill toward men!'"

The purpose of God sending Jesus into this world was to establish peace and goodwill between God and us.

The only thing that is precious and valuable to God on Earth are people (John 3:16). And it is for this very reason that God did everything He could possibly do to see mankind restored back to Him.

The word 'Gospel' simply means 'Good News'. Jesus bridged the gap between God and mankind, giving us access to God our Heavenly Father.

Ephesians 2:17-18
"And He (Jesus) *came and preached peace to you who were afar off and to those who were*

near. (18) For through Him we both have access by one Spirit to the Father." (Emphasis added)

According to Ephesians 3:12, *"In whom we have _____ and _____ with _____ through faith in Him"*.

This peace that Jesus came to bring is peace with _____, peace with _____ and peace with _____.

The Hebrew word for 'peace' is *'Shalom'*, which means *'wholeness and well being'*.

In John 14, Jesus said the world cannot give you this peace, neither can it take it away.

John 14:27
"Peace I leave with you, My peace I give to you; not as the world gives do I give to you. Let not your heart be troubled, neither let it be afraid."

Our Responsibility
God has now entrusted us with the responsibility of declaring this good news to the rest of the world.

Romans 10:14-15
"How then shall they call on Him in whom they have not believed? And how shall they believe in Him of whom they have not heard? And how shall they hear without a preacher? (15) And how shall they preach unless they are sent? ..."

You and I are chosen by God for a purpose, and our ministry is to reconcile man to God through the Gospel.

II Corinthians 5:18
"... God, who has reconciled us to Himself through Jesus Christ, and has given us the _____ of reconciliation".

Today, you have received the Gift of Salvation which has impacted your life ... because someone took this ministry seriously and shared the Gospel with you.

II Corinthians 5:20
"Now then, we are ambassadors for Christ, as though God were pleading through us: we implore you on Christ's behalf, be reconciled to God."

An 'Ambassador' is one who is a representative of another Nation. In the same way, we are chosen by God to be His Ambassadors, His representatives of His Kingdom, in a world which is ignorant of this truth.

The Apostle Paul took this ministry of reconciliation seriously, and pleaded with people on Christ's behalf, to be reconciled to (have peace with) God.

> II Timothy 2:20 - 23
> *"But in a great house there are not only vessels of gold and silver, but also of wood and clay, some for honour and some for dishonour. (21) Therefore if anyone cleanses himself from the latter, he will be a vessel for honour, sanctified and useful for the Master, prepared for every good work. (22) Flee also youthful lusts; but pursue righteousness, faith, love, peace with those who call on the Lord out of a pure heart. (23) But avoid _____ and _____ disputes, knowing that they generate strife."*

JESUS' MESSAGE

Because of Adam's sin, all of mankind were separated from God and His presence. In this fallen state, we continued to walk in rebellion towards God, which would have resulted in eternal destruction - Hell. The Bible says in Romans 6:23 that, *"The wages of sin is death, but the gift of God is eternal life in Christ Jesus our Lord"*. Jesus stood in our place, paid the penalty for our sins by dying on the cross, so that you and I could be saved. The Greek word for 'Salvation' is *'Sozo'* (sōzō), which means *'to save, to deliver, to protect, heal, preserve, do well, make whole'*. This tells us that our salvation is not just about our sins being forgiven, but it is also about God's heart to heal, deliver, make us whole and protect us.

The good news is that God has made provision for every sinner to be forgiven of all the sins he/she has ever committed, giving every individual the opportunity to receive God's forgiveness by faith, so that he/she can now experience salvation.

Salvation is God's gift to us - it is something we cannot earn. The Bible tells us in Ephesians 2:8-9, that it is *"By grace you have been saved through faith, and that not of yourselves; it is the gift of God. (9) not of works, lest anyone should boast"*.

OUR MISSION

There are two things that Jesus said concerning our mission on Earth. They are:

a) We are His Salt and His Light in this World

> Matthew 5:13 -16
> *"You are the _____ of the earth; but if the salt loses its flavour, how shall it be seasoned? It is then good for nothing but to be thrown out and trampled underfoot by men. (14) You are the _____ of the world. A city that is set on a hill cannot be hidden. (15) Nor do they light a lamp and put it under a basket, but on a*

*lampstand, and it gives light to all who are in the house. (16) _____
so shine before men, that they may see your good works and glorify your Father in heaven."*

Salt and Light are two things that we cannot do without in this World. Salt and Light are significant in themselves because of what they contribute. Our food would be tasteless if Salt was not added to it. And our lives would be directionless (groping in the darkness), if there was no Light.

You become His Salt to the people around you once you have the Spirit of Jesus living in you - You begin to add flavour to in the lives of people, which is unfortunately otherwise absent in the world today.

C. S. Lewis said, *"Education without values, as useful as it is, seems rather to make man a more clever devil".*

It is Godly character that will make this World a better place. God is counting on us to play our part in seeing us spread the flavour of His peace, His freedom, His love to others.

Similarly, God has called each one of us to be His Light in this dark world. People in this world are looking for answers to their problems; there are thousands of people who lack direction and purpose in life; they just exist to eat and work, living their lives to gratify their desires, and God has called us to be His Light, pointing them in the right direction.

And when you live a righteous life, your mouth will be filled with wisdom and justice.

Psalm 37:30-31

_____
_____

---

b) His mandate

Mark 16:15-18
"And He said to them, 'Go into all the world and preach the gospel to every creature. (16) He who believes and is baptised will be saved; but he who does not believe will be condemned. (17) And these signs will follow those who believe: In My name they will cast out demons; they will speak with new tongues; (18) they will take up serpents; and if they drink anything deadly, it will by no means hurt them; they will lay hands on the sick, and they will recover.'"

> What are the three signs that follow a person who believes in Christ?
> 1. _____
> 2. _____
> 3. _____

Mark 16:19-20
"So then, after the Lord had spoken to them, He was received up into heaven, and sat down at the right hand of God. (20) And they went out and preached everywhere, the Lord working with them and confirming the word through the accompanying signs."

God has great plans for His people. The Bible says in Romans 8:32, *"He who did not spare His own Son, but delivered Him up for us all, how shall He not with Him also freely give us all things?"*

God wants us to yield our bodies as instruments of righteousness, so that He could fulfil His plans through us.

Romans 6:19 (NIV)
"... Just as you used to offer yourselves as slaves to impurity and to ever-increasing wickedness, so now offer yourselves as slaves to righteousness leading to holiness".

We must first become the servants of His righteousness, before we become the servants of the Lord.

God wants to heal and deliver those who are suffering and those who are in bondage, and He wants to eradicate poverty and corruption - but, He can only accomplish this task through you and me. The only thing we have that God does not have is a physical body - and that is why, since the beginning of creation, God always searched for a person through whom He could fulfil His plans. Even the coming of our Saviour happened only when Mary, a willing vessel, said *"Yes"* to God. **Therefore, we must be equipped and ready to share the Gospel.**

> Just as boots protect the feet of a soldier at war, in a similar manner, the Gospel of Peace is important for us since it provides protection from the enemy and prepares us to fulfil His mandate. In a time of war, a soldier never takes off his boots, even when he rests - he is always prepared for action. In the same way, we should always be equipped with the Gospel of Peace - be ready for action.

PERSONAL REFLECTION

Why is it important for us to share the Gospel?
_____
_____

What does your ministry of reconciliation involve?
_____
_____

MEMRY VERSE

"...*who desires all men to be saved and to come to the knowledge of the truth*."

I Timothy 2:4

To live in the power and demonstration of the Gospel

REVIEW OF LESSON IV (PART I)

Having been reconciled with God, what is the ministry that you have been chosen for? (II Corinthians 5:18)
_____

God wants us to yield our bodies as instruments of _____, so that He could fulfil His plans through us.

Why should our feet be prepared with the Gospel of Peace?
_____
_____

How did you apply Lesson IV (Part I) in your life?
_____
_____

Write down the memory verse you learnt last week?
_____
_____

Determination (Faith) + Discipline = Growth

LESSON IV
THE GOSPEL OF PEACE

PART II
ESTABLISHING YOURSELF IN THE GOSPEL

"For I am not ashamed of the gospel of Christ, for it is the power of God to salvation ...".
- Romans 1:16

It is important for you to be established in the Gospel before you start sharing the Gospel. The Bible tells us that, *"The message of the cross is foolishness to those who are perishing, but to us who are being saved it is the power of God"* (I Corinthians 1:18). The Gospel is the power of God to those who believe in Jesus' death, resurrection and ascension, but it is foolishness to those who do not believe.

The Apostle Paul said in Romans 1:16, *"For I am not ashamed of the gospel of Christ, for it is the power of God to salvation for everyone who _____, for the Jew first and also for the Greek"*.

No one is born a Christian; but we can all be born-again Christians when we believe what God has done for us through His Son, Jesus.

The five things that we must believe about the Gospel are as follows:

1. GOD LOVES YOU ... EVEN WHEN YOU WERE A SINNER!

John 3:16 -17
"For God so loved the world that He gave His only begotten Son, that whoever _____ in Him should not perish but have everlasting life. (17) For God did not send His Son into the world to _____ the world, but that the world through Him might be _____."

Romans 5:7-8 (NIV)
"Very rarely will anyone die for a righteous person, though for a good person someone might possibly dare to die. (8) But God demonstrates his own love for us in this: While we were still sinners, Christ died for us."

You don't get rid of all your sins before you come to Christ; but, you come to Christ because He can forgive you and cleanse you from all your sins. We come to God all messed up and unclean, but as we continue to trust in Him, He cleanses us and delivers us from our bondage to sin.

In John 15:9, Jesus said, *"As the Father loved me,* **I also have loved you***; abide in my love".*

2. SIN SEPARATES YOU FROM GOD

Romans 3:23
"For _____ have sinned and fall short of the glory of God, ... ".

We don't sin and then become sinners; we are born in sin, and are therefore prone to sin. Sin separated us from God. And so, man in his sinful state began searching for God. All religion is about man's efforts to reach God. But, Christianity is about God reaching out to us through His Son, Jesus.

Isaiah 59:1-2 (NIV)
"Surely the arm of the Lord is _____ too short to save, nor his ear too dull to hear. (2) But your iniquities (sin) *have separated you from your God; your sins have hidden his face from you, so that he will not hear."* (Emphasis added)

Write down some of the things you did to earn God's acceptance and forgiveness before you came to Christ.
_____

---

3. JESUS IS GOD'S ONLY PROVISION FOR YOUR SIN

Christianity is about God searching for man to be reunited with Him.

I Timothy 2:5
"For there is one God and _____ Mediator between God and men, the Man Christ Jesus."
Acts 4:12 (ESV)
" ... for there is no other name under heaven given among men by which we must be saved".

Hebrews 10:17-18
*"Their sins and their lawless deeds I will remember _____. (8)
Now where there is remission* (the cancellation of a debt, charge, or penalty) *of these, there is no longer an offering for sin".* (Emphasis added)

4. JESUS IS ALIVE AND HE IS THE ONLY WAY TO GOD

The resurrection of Jesus is the very heart of Christianity - it is the central part of the Gospel. If Jesus had not resurrected from the dead, then all our faith in Him would be in vain.

Acts 10:39-40 (NIV)
"We are witnesses of everything he did in the country of the Jews and in Jerusalem. They killed him by hanging him on a cross, (40) but God raised him from the dead on the third day and caused him to be seen."

Acts 13:34
"And that He raised Him from the dead, no more to return to corruption ... ".

The founders of other religions are dead; they no longer live. While, Jesus, who existed at the very beginning of creation, not only rose from the dead, but is now alive and qualifies to be the only way to God.

John 14:6
"Jesus said to him, 'I am the way, the truth, and the life. _____ comes to the Father except through Me'."

John 10:9
"I am the door. If _____ enters by Me, he will be saved, and will go in and out and find pasture."

We don't worship a dead Saviour ... we worship the resurrected Lord!

5. YOU MUST KNOW GOD PERSONALLY

A man named Nicodemus came to see Jesus at night because he feared that his reputation would be at stake if others knew he had come to see Jesus. Nicodemus was a Pharisee who belonged to a very religious group who believed in following a strict set of rules to be righteous. Even though he was such a pious man, Jesus said in John 3:5-7, *"... unless one is born of water and the Spirit, he cannot enter the kingdom of God. (6) That which is born of the flesh is flesh, and that which is born of the Spirit is spirit. (7) Do not marvel that I said to you, 'You must be born again'."*
The decision to be born-again, to be united with God, so that one can have fellowship with Him, must be an individual choice. And this experience of being born-again is what **salvation** is all about.

Ephesians 2:8-9
"For by grace you have been saved through faith, and that not of yourselves; it is the gift of God, (9) not of works, lest anyone should boast."

Revelation 3:20
"Behold, I stand at the door and knock. If anyone hears My voice and opens the door, I will come in to him and dine with him, and he with Me."

When you establish yourself in the truth of the Gospel, you will not only live in the good of the Gospel, but you will also be effective in sharing the Gospel.

PERSONAL REFLECTION

When you've experienced something good, it is only natural that you tell others about it. God gave you a testimony so that you could share it with others.

What did you experience when you accepted Christ as your Saviour?

_____

_____

_____

Write down your testimony in three simple steps (this will help you to share the Gospel effectively):

1. Your life before Christ (briefly)
2. How and when you experienced Christ in your life
3. The changes you saw after your salvation

MEMRY VERSE

"For I am not ashamed of the gospel of Christ, for it is the power of God to salvation for everyone who believes, for the Jew first and also for the Greek."

Romans 1:16

Find people with whom you can share the Gospel and disciple them.

REVIEW OF LESSON IV (PART II)

What are the five main aspects of the Gospel?

1. _____

2. _____

3. _____

4. _____

5. _____

How did you apply Lesson IV (Part II) in your life?
_____
_____

Write down the memory verse you learnt last week?
_____
_____

Determination (Faith) + Discipline = Growth

LESSON V
THE SHIELD OF FAITH

"Above all, taking the shield of faith with which you will be able to quench all the fiery darts of the wicked one."
- Ephesians 6:16

Every Christian is in a spiritual battle against Satan and his kingdom. Satan's agenda is to always oppose everything that is Godly. According to the above verse, he is known as the *"wicked one"* and his temptations are like *"fiery darts"* meant to destroy us. When somebody shoots a fiery dart at you, it is obvious that their intention is to destroy or kill you. For this reason, the Bible says, *"above all, take the shield of faith"*. In other words, the Belt of Truth, the Breastplate of Righteousness and the Gospel of Peace are not sufficient for you to quench (extinguish, put out) the *"fiery darts of the wicked one"*; you need faith as your shield.

We may have the first 3 pieces of the Armour, but if we don't have Faith as our Shield, then we can be so easily destroyed by the *"wicked one"* (Satan). Temptations are more than just a negative thought or a concept in our minds; temptations are spiritual attacks from the wicked one who aims to destroy us.

In Matthew 4, we see how Jesus handled temptation. He recognised Satan as the tempter and did not just rebuke the wicked thought, but He also rebuked Satan who was behind the temptations.

Satan knew that Jesus had been fasting for 40 days, and so he chose the most vulnerable time in Jesus' life to tempt Him … and that is how Satan works. He knows our weaknesses, and so when our defences are down, he uses our weaknesses to lure us into his trap, and attacks us.

For example, if potato chips/crisps are your weakness, then it is very likely that you will fall into that temptation when you see them. But, if chocolates are not your weakness, then it is foolish to tempt you with a chocolate. Therefore, if someone wants to tempt you, they first need to know what your weaknesses are. Similarly, if sex, money, pride, selfish-ambition, etc., are your weaknesses, then there are chances of the *"wicked one"* (Satan) tempting you in those areas.

James 4:7
"Therefore submit to God. Resist the devil and he will flee from you."

When you bring your thoughts in submission to God's Word and then resist the enemy, he will flee from you.

It is for this reason that Jesus taught us to pray in Matthew 6:13, *"And do not lead us into temptation, but deliver us from the evil one"*. The phrase *"lead us not into temptation"* speaks of Jesus protecting and delivering us from temptation.

Jesus knew what we would be up against - Satan and his temptations; so, He prayed for us before He ascended into Heaven, *"I do not pray that You should take them out of the world, but that You should keep them from the evil one"* (John 17:15).

Even the Apostle Paul referred to Satan as the tempter.

I Thessalonians 3:5
"For this reason, when I could no longer endure it, I sent to know your faith, lest by some means the _____ had _____ you, and our labor might be in vain."

The Psalmist who fought many battles probably understood this more than anyone else. He knew what it meant to have God as his Shield.

Psalm 3:3
"But You, O LORD, are a shield for me, my glory and the One who lifts up my head."

In Genesis 15:1, God revealed Himself in a vision to Abraham and said, *"... Do not be afraid, Abram. **I am your shield,** your exceedingly great reward"*.

Faith in Jesus is our shield that nullifies the fiery darts of the enemy. This piece of the Armour is for our defence against the wicked one.

Jude 1:24
"Now to Him (Jesus) *who is able to keep you from stumbling, and to present you faultless before the presence of His glory with exceeding joy."* (Emphasis added)

Who is able to keep you from falling?

_____

It is important to know that even Jesus, when He was in the flesh, depended on His Father to protect Him from falling into temptation.

Hebrews 5:7-8
"Who, in the days of His flesh, when He had offered up prayers and supplications, with vehement cries and tears to Him who was able to save Him from death, and was heard because of His godly fear, (8) though He was a Son, yet He learned obedience by the things which He suffered."

In the following verse, what did Jesus do when people hurled insults at Him?

I Peter 2:23 (NIV)
"When they hurled their insults at him, he did not retaliate; when he suffered, he made no threats. Instead, he _____ who judges justly."

Hebrews 4:14-16
"Seeing then that we have a great High Priest who has passed through the heavens, Jesus the Son of God, let us hold fast our confession. (15) For we do not have a High Priest who cannot sympathise with our weaknesses, but was in all points tempted as we are, yet without sin. (16) Let us therefore come boldly to the throne of grace, that we may obtain mercy and find grace to help in time of need."

According to Hebrews 4, who is your High Priest?
_____

What does Jesus do when you are tempted?
_____

How should you approach the Throne of Grace?
_____

What do you receive?
_____

We all deserved to be punished, because of our sinful ways; but, Jesus took that punishment on the cross so that He could demonstrate mercy to us. **Mercy** is getting what you don't deserve. On the other hand, **grace** is divine ability; when we come with confidence before God, He gives us the ability to overcome every kind of temptation.

Take courage that you are not alone in all your temptations. The Bible tells us that we have One who was just like us, One who endured every kind of temptation and is now in Heaven interceding for us.

Our confidence in Jesus acts as our Shield, and this is what protects us from falling into temptation. Therefore, let Jesus be your Shield. Trust Him.

Hebrews 3:6
" ... but Christ as a Son over His own house, whose house we are if we hold fast the confidence and the rejoicing of the hope firm to the end".

> **MY JOURNAL**
>
> *"In my early days, I struggled with an emotional battle concerning a person of the opposite sex, who used to send me prayer requests along with "I love you" messages. There were times I would wake up in the middle of the night with the fear that I was giving into my emotions. I came to a place where my emotions began to over-ride my judgement. At this point, I found that I could no longer handle this by myself. I poured out my heart to God, telling Him how vulnerable I was. And it was during this time that Jude 1:24 became a reality in my life.*
>
> *The Bible says, "Now to Him who is able to keep you from stumbling, and to present you faultless before the presence of His glory with exceeding joy" (Jude 1:24).*
>
> *I shared this struggle with a Pastor friend of mine. Just talking to him helped me bring closure to what I was going through. Miraculously, all the cards and prayer requests with the "I love you" notes stopped.*
>
> *Since then, to date, this verse has been the cornerstone in my life. If we remain faithful to the Lord until the end, it will only be because He keeps us from falling. And it is Jesus who presents us faultless before the presence of God's exceeding glory."*

Whether it is the assurance of our salvation, pride, sexual temptation, any ungodly relationship, etc., that you may be caught in, always remember that it is your trust in Jesus which will keep you from falling. Jesus wants you to live an overcomer's life, and He is interceding for you.

> A shield protects a soldier from the attacks of the enemy. In the same way, your faith is a shield that protects you from every attack of the enemy.

PERSONAL REFLECTION

What is it that you are struggling with? And in what way are you trusting Jesus to keep you from falling into this temptation?

If this is an on-going struggle, you could consider sharing this with someone who can disciple you in this area. (It takes faith to share your struggles with someone.)

MEMRY VERSE

"For the Scripture says, 'Whoever believes on Him will not be put to shame.'"

Romans 10:11

Shield of Faith

G⊙AL

To be an overcomer with regards to every temptation that comes my way.

REVIEW OF LESSON V

According to Hebrews 4:14-16, what does Jesus do?
_____
_____

And what is our responsibility?
_____
_____

_____ in Jesus is our shield that nullifies the fiery darts of the enemy.

How did you apply Lesson V in your life?
_____
_____

Write down the memory verse you learnt last week?
_____
_____

Determination (Faith) + Discipline = Growth

LESSON VI
THE HELMET OF SALVATION

"And take the helmet of salvation...".
- Ephesians 6:17

The Helmet of Salvation, unlike a metal helmet, is made up of the Scriptures, that are deeply embedded in our minds and hearts, and which protects us against negative thoughts and doubts.

Colossians 3:16 says, *"Let the word of Christ dwell in you richly in all wisdom ..."*. The word 'dwell' means *'to reside, to be settled, to be housed'*. God wants His Word to dwell (to be housed) in your minds, richly and in all wisdom.

Everything we see around us first started with a thought. And our mind is the pathway through which we get influenced. Therefore, it is essential that we guard our mind against any negative influence.

You received a new spirit when you were born-again, but you had the same old mind. So, guarding your mind is very important.

In all of our day-to-day activities, our minds are under constant attack from various sources such as the media, negative statements that we hear, the things we read, etc.. So, we need to guard our thoughts against being defiled, and from doubting our salvation or even God's love for us. Ephesians 6:17 instructs us to *"take the helmet of salvation"*. The Bible uses the word *"take"* as a reminder for us not to forget to '*take* our helmet'. The Helmet of Salvation protects us from these lies of the enemy.

The assurance of your salvation and your forgiveness is not based on your feelings, but on faith in what God's Word says.

I John 5:11-12
"And this is the testimony: that God has given us eternal life, and this life is in His Son. (12) He who has the Son has life; he who does not have the Son of God does not have life."

> What is eternal life?
>
> I John 5:20
> *"And we know that the Son of God has come and has given us an understanding, that we may know Him who is true; and we are in Him who is true, in His Son Jesus Christ. This is the true God and eternal life."*
>
> When do we have eternal life?
> When we accept Jesus.

Romans 12:2
"Do not be conformed to this world, but be transformed by the renewing of your mind, that you may prove what is that good and acceptable and perfect will of God."

The Bible uses the word *"transformed"*, speaking of transformation which is a process of 'metamorphosis' - *'a change of the form or nature of a thing or person into a completely different one'*. Just as a caterpillar transforms into a butterfly, we also are transformed by the renewing of our minds by the Word of God.

I Peter 1:13
"Therefore gird up the loins of your mind, be sober, and rest your hope fully upon the grace that is to be brought to you at the revelation of Jesus Christ."

The word *"loins"* refers to the reproductive area of our body. The Bible uses the word *"loins"* with regards to our mind, because the source of all our creativity and transformation starts with our thoughts. You and I will never get to believe God's promises unless we first perceive in our mind what He will do.

The Helmet of Salvation keeps you secure in God's steadfast love and acceptance because what you think is what you feel.

We are most vulnerable when it comes to our thoughts. The most indisciplined area of our lives are our thoughts, which constantly determine what we say and what we do. Our mind has been open to Satan's attack since the very beginning of time. Even right there in the Garden of Eden, Satan attacked Eve through her mind.

Therefore, the purpose for this Helmet of Salvation is to guard our thought life against thoughts of fear, hatred, unbelief, lust, etc..

> So, how do you guard your thoughts?
> By meditating on God's Word, memorising Scripture, making sure your mind is engaged in things that are positive (reading edifying books, playing sports, fellowshipping with the right people, etc.).

When you are tempted with negative and ungodly thoughts, your first response should be to take that negative thought captive. It is only when you dwell on the thought that the temptation gets unmanageable. The second helpful tip is to divert your thoughts onto something positive. We cannot change the environment in which we live; but, we can change our response to it.

Write down the two things that you must do when faced with temptation.

_____

_____

The Bible instructs us on how we can deal with the negative thoughts that have become strongholds in our mind.

> II Corinthians 10:4-5 (KJV)
> *"For the weapons of our warfare are not carnal, but mighty through God to the pulling down of strong holds; (5) casting down imaginations* (images)*, and every high thing that exalteth itself against the knowledge of God, and bringing into captivity every thought to the obedience of Christ; ... "*. (Emphasis added)

The word 'imagination' comes from the word image. Your thoughts create images in your mind, which can either build you up or pull you down. Just as fear creates a negative image in a person's mind, faith creates a positive image in our mind. Therefore, these negative images in our mind can be replaced with positive images by meditating on God's Word.

> Psalms 1:1-3
> *"Blessed is the man who walks not in the counsel of the ungodly, nor stands in the path of sinners, nor sits in the seat of the scornful; (2) but his delight is in the law of the Lord, and in His law he meditates day and night. (3) He shall be like a tree planted by the rivers of water, that brings forth its fruit in its season, whose leaf also shall not wither; and whatever he does shall prosper."*

The secret behind our prosperity is meditating on God's Word. The Greek word for the 'mind' is ὅλῃ τῇ διανοίᾳ σου - (dee-an'-oy-ah) - it is the same word for 'meditation'. We find this word being used many times throughout the New Testament, while referring to meditation.

> **Write down God's instruction to Joshua in Joshua 1:8.**
>
> _____
>
> _____

Every time you meditate on God's Word, it must create a positive image in your mind.

James 1:14-15
"But each one is tempted when he is drawn away by his own desires and enticed. (15) Then, when desire has conceived, it gives birth to sin; and sin, when it is full-grown, brings forth death."

It is important to realise that sin is first conceived in our mind before it becomes an action. What you think is what you feel. Therefore, you will never be able to control your feelings if you are not able to control your thinking.

Your thoughts need to be controlled by the Holy Spirit if you want to live a Spirit-filled life.

Romans 8:5 (AMPC)
"For those who are according to the flesh and are controlled by its unholy desires set their minds on and pursue those things which gratify the flesh, but those who are according to the Spirit and are controlled by the desires of the Spirit set their minds on and seek those things which gratify the [Holy] Spirit."

MY JOURNAL

"As a young Pastor, I had various verses from the Bible pinned up in my office, to remind me that if I wanted to live a life controlled by the Holy Spirit, then I had to yield my mind, by choice, to what pleased the Holy Spirit. I knew that if I thought right, I would not only feel right, but would also live right. I not only had these verses up in my office, I also pasted them on my mirror. My desire for the Holy Spirit to dwell in me was what motivated me to make Godly choices in the midst of temptations."

I Corinthians 6:19-20
"Or do you not know that your body is the temple of the Holy Spirit who is in you, whom you have from God, and you are not your own? (20) For you were bought at a price; therefore glorify God in your body and in your spirit, which are God's."

Just as a couple makes a marriage vow binding them to each another, in like manner, you now belong to no one else but to God and the Holy Spirit.

> Your head is the source of command from where your body receives instructions. This is why protecting your head is so vital. In the physical world, we have helmets to protect our head; similarly, the Helmet of Salvation equips your 'control room', enabling you to function effectively.

PERSONAL REFLECTION

Are you able to guard your thought life from the lies of the enemy?

Write down three negative images that control your emotions and behaviour in a negative way.

1. _____
2. _____
3. _____

Write down verses that would create a positive image in your mind and would help replace the negative image.

Philippians 4:8
"Finally, brethren, whatever things are true, whatever things are noble, whatever things are just, whatever things are pure, whatever things are lovely, whatever things are of good report, if there is any virtue and if there is anything praiseworthy—meditate on these things."

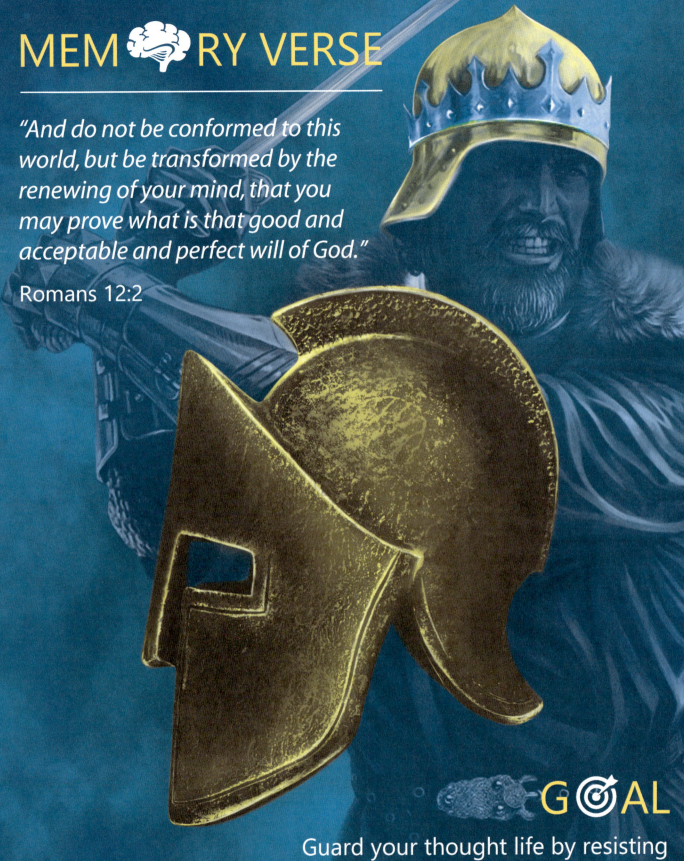

MEMORY VERSE

"And do not be conformed to this world, but be transformed by the renewing of your mind, that you may prove what is that good and acceptable and perfect will of God."

Romans 12:2

GOAL

Guard your thought life by resisting every temptation that the enemy puts in your mind. Take the first thought captive!

REVIEW OF LESSON VI

The assurance of your salvation and your forgiveness is not based on your feelings, but is based on what _____ says.

The purpose for the Helmet of Salvation is to _____ from thoughts of fear, hatred, unbelief, thoughts of lust, etc..

Sin is first _____ in our mind before it becomes an action.

How did you apply Lesson VI in your life?
_____
_____

Write down the memory verse you learnt last week?
_____
_____

Determination (Faith) + Discipline = Growth

LESSON VII
THE SWORD OF THE SPIRIT

"For the word of God is living and powerful, and sharper than any two-edged sword, piercing even to the division of soul and spirit, and of joints and marrow, and is a discerner of the thoughts and intents of the heart.".
- Hebrews 4:12

The Sword of the Holy Spirit is the only piece of the Armour which is given for our offensive attack against Satan and his works. It was this weapon that Jesus used when He was tempted in the wilderness.

Ephesians 6:17b
"...and the Sword of the Spirit, which is the Word of God".

God does not want us to be passive and timid Christians. We need to take courage and use this weapon to stand against every scheme of the enemy that the Devil uses to pull us down.

I John 3:7-9 (ESV)
"Little children, let no one deceive you. Whoever practices righteousness is righteous, as he is righteous. (8) Whoever makes a practice of sinning is of the devil, for the devil has been sinning from the beginning. **The reason the Son of God appeared was to destroy the works of the devil.** *(9) No one born of God makes a practice of sinning, for God's seed abides in him; and he cannot keep on sinning, because he has been born of God."*

Sin is spiritual, and it's origin is from the Devil. Therefore, it is important to know that the purpose of Jesus' death was not only to die on the cross for our sins, but was to also destroy the works of the Devil.

Read Matthew 4 and fill in the blanks as to how Jesus resisted the temptations of the Devil.

According to verse 3, Satan is known as the _____. In verse 4, Jesus answered and said, "_____, 'Man shall not live by bread alone, but by *every word that proceeds from the mouth of God'."*

In verse 7, what did Jesus do? He said, "_____, *'You shall not tempt the Lord your God'."*

> **In verse 8 and 9, what did the Devil tempt Jesus to do, and how did Jesus respond in verse 10?**
>
> _____
> _____
> _____
> _____

Jesus set us an example showing us how we too can deal with the Devil's temptations, and be victorious.

Note:
While dealing with temptations, Jesus not only dealt with the deceptive thoughts and words of the Devil, but He also rebuked Satan himself. Therefore, you too will have more victories than defeat when you deal with temptations in like manner.

The Bible refers to the Word of God as a two-edged sword that divides between the soul and spirit, our thoughts and our intentions (attitudes).

> Hebrews 4:12 (ESV)
> *"For the word of God is living and active, sharper than any two-edged sword, piercing to the division of soul and of spirit, of joints and of marrow, and discerning the thoughts and intentions of the heart."*

The Word of God helps us discern between the thoughts in our soul (our mind, our will and our emotions) and the attitudes and intentions in our human spirit. The Holy Spirit convicts us of sin and speaks to us through our human spirit.

Most of us enjoy times of worship or even praying, but not many like spending time with the Word of God on a regular basis. Remember, the Word of God (Bible) is the weapon of the Holy Spirit, which gives us our victory over sin and the works of the Devil.

We must therefore cultivate a habit of not only spending time with God in worship and prayer, but also spend time with the Word of God everyday. Every time you speak the Word of God in faith, knowing that you stand righteous in God's presence, the Word of God goes forth like a sword from your mouth to destroy the enemy.

We need to cultivate a habit of spending time with God and His Word if we are to be overcomers. Revelation 3:5 says, *"He who _____ shall be clothed in white garments, and I will not blot out his name from the Book of Life; but I will confess his name before My Father and before His angels".*

It is not how we start our Christian life that matters, but how we finish.

Very often, we try and fight temptation in our own ability, and fail. If we could only have lived a righteous life in our own strength, then God would not have sent Jesus to save us from our sins.

Jesus overcame every temptation because He was equipped with the full Armour.

>I Corinthians 10:12
>*"Therefore let him who thinks he stands take heed lest he _____."*

The purpose of Jesus' coming into this World was to show us how we could live a victorious life in a fallen world.

>Jesus was girded with the **Belt of Truth**, because He knew the Father, and knew who He was.
>Jesus had the **Breastplate of Righteousness**, because in Him there was no sin.
>His feet were equipped with the preparation of the **Gospel of Peace** as He went demonstrating the Kingdom of Heaven and healing the sick.
>He walked continuously with the **Shield of Faith**, with total dependence in the Father.
>He had the **Helmet of Salvation** and never doubted that He was the Son of God who had come to save mankind from their sins.
>He used the **Sword of the Spirit** and spoke with wisdom and authority.

This Armour is not something we put on and then take off, **but is an Armour that represents spiritual truths that we must live in always.** Therefore, if you and I are going to walk in victory, we need to be fully clad with the Armour of Jesus.

In the physical world we are just ordinary human beings, but in the spiritual realm we are armed with Jesus, from head to toe. The Armour of God positions us in a place of spiritual authority to overcome every temptation, sin and the deceptive ways of the enemy.

You become an overcomer when you have put on the whole Armour of God.

>Romans 13:12b
>*"... Therefore let us cast off the works of darkness, and let us put on the armour of light".*

The full Armour of Jesus positions us to stand with boldness and confidence before Almighty God.

> Ephesians 3:12
> *"In whom* (Christ) *we have _____ and _____ _____ with confidence through faith in Him* (Jesus Christ).*"* (Emphasis added)

For most people, their prayer time is only about expressing their feelings to God, and that is not wrong - when you only express your feelings to God, you receive comfort; but, when you pray using the Scripture, you are praying for results. You would have probably noticed that every time Jesus prayed it was never silent. It is interesting to note that while in prayer, Jesus always spoke to His Heavenly Father, but when He spoke to the Devil, He used the Word of God as a Sword to fulfil its purpose.

Salvation is not only about you believing in your heart, but it is also about you speaking with your mouth.

Cultivate the habit of speaking the truth over your life - it will have a transforming effect on your life and circumstances.

> Proverbs 18:21
> *"Death and life are in the power of the _____, and those who love it will eat its fruit."*

If we want to be victorious, we need to be equipped with the full armour of God, just the way Jesus was, while He was on Earth.

> II Timothy 3:16-17
> *"All Scripture is given by inspiration of God, and is profitable for doctrine, for reproof, for correction, for instruction in righteousness, (17) that the man of God may be complete, thoroughly equipped for every good work."*

The only weapon of attack that a soldier uses is the sword, which can destroy the enemy. In like manner, the Sword of the Spirit is the one weapon that we have which can destroy the work of the enemy. Every soldier practices the art of using his sword effectively. In the same way, we too must be fully equipped to handle the Word of God in order to gain victory over the enemy.

MEMORY VERSE

"This Book of the Law shall not depart from your mouth, but you shall meditate in it day and night, that you may observe to do according to all that is written in it. For then you will make your way prosperous, and then you will have good success."

Joshua 1:8

GOAL

Cultivate the habit of reading and meditating on God's Word daily.

REVIEW OF LESSON VII

I need to gird myself with the _____, knowing who my Heavenly Father is, wear the _____, because I am made righteous in Christ. My feet should be equipped with the _____ to be effective in sharing the Gospel of Salvation. I must always use the _____ to protect me from the plots and plans of the enemy. The _____ is what protects me from doubt and temptations. And above all, the _____ _____ which is the Word of God enables me to walk in victory!

How did you apply Lesson VII in your life?
_____
_____

Write down the memory verse you learnt last week?
_____
_____

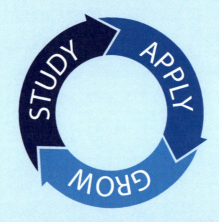

Determination (Faith) + Discipline = Growth

LESSON VIII
DEVOTIONAL LIFE

"God is faithful, by whom you were called into the fellowship of His Son, Jesus Christ our Lord.".
- I Corinthians 1:9

God desires to have fellowship with you every day. He wants to speak to you personally through the Bible and He wants you to speak to Him through prayer. And it is for this very reason that Jesus came into this world to restore our **relationship** and **fellowship** with God.

A devotional time is when a person sets aside time on a daily basis, where he/she spends his/her time exclusively with God.

> I Corinthians 1:9
> *"God is _____, by whom you were called into the _____ of His Son, Jesus Christ our Lord."*

Listed below are some of the reasons why we should cultivate the habit of spending time with God.

God is our Heavenly Father, and we were created to have fellowship with Him.

> Genesis 3:8-9
> *"Then the man and his wife heard the sound of the LORD God as he was walking in the garden in the cool of the day, and they hid from the LORD God among the trees of the garden. (9) But the LORD God called to the man, 'Where are you?'"*

Even though Adam and Eve rebelled against God and hid from Him, it was God who took the initiative to seek after them and to reach out to them.

The most significant revelation we have in the New Testament is about God being our Heavenly Father. Jesus taught His disciples to pray in Matthew 6:9, *"... Our Father in heaven, Hallowed be Your name"*.

Matthew 7:11
"If you then, being evil, know how to give good gifts to your children, _____ _____ will your Father who is in heaven _____ to those who ask Him!"

We make the biggest mistake when we compare God to our earthly fathers. God, our Heavenly Father, surpasses every human expectation of our earthly fathers. Even as you look to God as your Heavenly Father, He looks at you as His child.

Galatians 4:6
"And because you are sons, God has sent forth the Spirit of His Son into your hearts, crying out, 'Abba, Father!'"

Jesus' source of power and wisdom came from His time spent with God.

Mark 1:35 (NIV)
"Very early in the morning, while it was still dark, Jesus got up, left the house and went off to a solitary place, where he prayed."

Luke 22:39-40 (NIV)
"Jesus went out _____ to the Mount of Olives, and his disciples followed him. (40) On reaching the place, he said to them, 'Pray that you will not fall into temptation'."

Luke 5:16
" ... Jesus _____ withdrew to lonely places and prayed ... ".

Your devotional time, should not be to just study about Christ, but it should also be to spend time with Him (apart from your family devotion time).

The following are practical guidelines that will help you to spend time with God.

a) Spend time in Worship
A good place to start is by spending time in worshipping God. Worship is about acknowledging God for who He is. We have already looked at Exodus 34, which describes God's Glory or Character. The different ways we get to know the Character of God are through His Creation, through the Bible and through the worship songs we sing.

You begin to trust others only as you get to know them; similarly, when you get to know God, it becomes easier for you to believe Him. This is how you grow in your faith.

Hebrews 11:6
"But without faith, it is impossible to please Him, for he who comes to God _____ _____, and that He is a _____ of those who diligently seek _____."

b) Giving Praise to God

Praise is thanking God for what He does, and it is good to express your gratitude to your Heavenly Father in praise. God has done so many good things for you - don't take these things for granted.

> Psalm 100:4
> *"Enter into His gates with thanksgiving, and into His courts with praise. Be thankful to Him, and bless His name."*

The Psalmist encouraged people to come into God's presence with an attitude of praise, because praise prepares our heart for worship.

> Hebrews 13:15
> *"Through Jesus, therefore, let us _____ offer to God a sacrifice of praise—the fruit of _____ that openly profess his name."*

> I Thessalonians 5:16-18
> *"Rejoice always, (17) pray without ceasing, (18) in everything give thanks; for this is the will of God in Christ Jesus for you."*

c) Prayer and Supplication

Supplication is about bringing your anxieties and petitions to God. The Bible encourages us to come to God before His Throne of Grace with confidence, so that you and I may receive His mercy and grace at the time of our need. God wants you to trust Him for all your needs.

> Hebrews 4:16 (NIV)
> *"Let us then approach the throne of grace with _____, so that we may _____ mercy and find grace to help us in our time of need."*

Mercy is what we receive by faith, based on who He is, when we come before God.

What does our Heavenly Father promise us when we come to Him?

Matthew 7:8

_____

_____

Matthew 7:11

_____

_____

The Apostle James says we fail to have what we need because we do not _____ _____ (James 4:2).

In I Peter 5:7, the Bible encourages you to cast ALL your cares, anxiety, worries on Him because God _____ for you.

> I Peter 5:7-8
> *"Casting all your cares* (anxiety, worries) *upon Him, for He cares for you. (8) Be sober, be vigilant; because your adversary the devil walks about like a roaring lion, seeking whom he may devour."* (Emphasis added)

You continue to worry because you are not confident that God cares for you and for what you are going through in life. The Bible encourages you to be serious and determined when you are trusting God with your worries, because if you do not, then the enemy will seek to devour you.

Spending time with God gives you the opportunity to share your innermost struggles, challenges and emotions with God, knowing that He is the only One who knows exactly what you are going through in life.

Read Matthew 6:25-34 and write down the things that your Heavenly Father does not want you to worry about?

1. _____
2. _____
3. _____
4. _____

Remember, **the only thing that pleases our Heavenly Father is faith** (and not doubt).

Jesus taught His disciples how to pray effectively:

> Mark 11:22-25 (ESV)
> *"And Jesus answered them, 'Have faith in God (23) Truly, I say to you, whoever says to this mountain, be taken up and thrown into the sea,' and does _____ in his heart, but _____ that what he says will come to pass, it will be done for him. (24) Therefore I tell you, whatever you ask in prayer, _____ _____, and it will be yours (25) And whenever you stand praying, forgive, if you have anything against anyone, so that your Father also who is in heaven may forgive you your trespasses'."*

Faith is about you first believing, before you receive an answer to your prayer.

Philippians 4:6
"Do not be anxious about _____, but in everything by prayer and _____ with _____ let your requests be made known to God."

d) Meditating on the Word of God
Before you start reading the Bible, ask the Holy Spirit (He is the Author of the Word of God) to reveal His Word to you.

Cultivate the habit of reading the Bible systematically everyday. (For example, if you are reading the Gospels, try and read a chapter each day.) When you read the Bible, make a note of what God is speaking to you through the passage; ask yourself the following questions:

- *"What do I understand **about God** from this passage?"*
- *"What do I understand **about man** from this passage?"*
- *"How should I respond if I find myself in the given situation?"*

Whenever God speaks to you through His Word, you must act on what you hear from Him.

James 1:22 (NIV)
"Do not merely listen to the word, and so deceive yourselves. Do what it says."

Read Luke 10:38-42 and fill in the blanks:

What did Mary do?

_____
_____

What prevented Martha from spending time with Jesus? (Verse 41)

_____
_____

What did Jesus say about Mary?

_____
_____

> What time and place did Jesus choose to spend time alone with His Father?
> _____
> _____
>
> Psalms 5:3 (NIV)
> *"In the morning, O LORD, you hear my voice; in the morning I lay my requests before you and wait in expectation."*
>
> According to Psalm 5:3, when is a good time to meet with the Lord each day?
> _____
> _____

Consider writing down the time and place where you will spend time with God no matter what the circumstances are.

Place : _____

Time : _____

BENEFITS OF SPENDING TIME WITH GOD:

To get direction from God

Psalm 25:4-5 (NIV)
"Show me your ways, O LORD, teach me your paths; (5) guide me in your truth and teach me, for you are God my Saviour, and my hope is in you all day long."

Proverbs 3:5-7 (ESV)
*"Trust in the LORD with all your heart and lean not on your own understanding; (6) in all your ways acknowledge him, _____.
(7) Do not be wise in your own eyes; fear the LORD and shun evil."*

The three steps that guarantee God guiding you are:

- Trust in the Lord with _____ your heart
- Lean not on _____ understanding
- In _____ your ways (circumstances) acknowledge _____
- He will direct your paths straight

Psalm 16:11
"You will show me the _____ of life; in Your presence is fullness of joy; at Your right hand are pleasures forevermore."

To become more like God

II Corinthians 3:18 (NIV)
"And we, who with unveiled faces all reflect the Lord's glory, are being transformed into his likeness with ever-increasing glory, which comes from the Lord, who is the Spirit."

What you behold, is what you become.

Transformation comes by gazing (not performing). Gazing is about us reflecting on His character in worship. The more we focus on who God is, the greater are the chances of our lives being transformed.

To grow in faith
Example - Abraham

Romans 4:20-21 (NIV)
"Yet he did not waver through _____ regarding the promise of God, but was strengthened in his _____ and gave glory to God, (21) being fully _____ that God had power to do what he had promised."

For wisdom

Matthew 7:24 (NIV)
"Therefore everyone who hears these words of mine and _____ is like a _____ who built his house on the rock."

For prosperity and success

Joshua 1:8
"This Book of the Law shall not depart from your _____, but you shall _____ in it day and night, that you may _____ to do according to all that is written in it. For then you will make your way prosperous, and then you will have good success."

Psalms 1:1-3
"Blessed is the man who does not walk in the counsel of the wicked or stand in the way of sinners or sit in the seat of mockers. (2) But his delight is in the law of the LORD, and on his law he meditates day and night. (3) He is like a tree planted by streams of water, which

yields its fruit in season and whose leaf does not wither. Whatever he does prospers."

For victory over sin

Psalm 119:9
"How can a young man keep his way pure? By living according to your word."

Psalm 119:11
"I have hidden your word in my _____ that I might not _____ against you."

"The Bible will keep you from sin, or sin will keep you from the Bible."
- Dwight L. Moody

> Your fellowship with God must be a two-way communication. When you pray, it is you speaking to God, but when you read the Word of God, it is God speaking to you.

PERSONAL REFLECTION

Is your devotional time just a routine, or does it enhance your relationship with God?

Are you actively believing God for what He has promised you?

Why don't you take a moment and thank God for all the times He has spoken to you.

MEMRY VERSE

"…casting all your care upon Him, for He cares for you. (8) Be sober, be vigilant; because your adversary the devil walks about like a roaring lion, seeking whom he may devour."

I Peter 5:7-8

G◎AL

To be free from anxiety, knowing that God cares for you.

REVIEW OF LESSON VIII

Jesus died so that our _____ and _____ with God was restored.

The only thing that pleases our Heavenly Father is _____

Whenever God speaks to you through His Word, you must _____ on what you hear.

Write down the benefits that you will have when you spend time with God.
_____
_____

How did you apply Lesson VIII in your life?
_____
_____

Write down the memory verse you learnt last week?
_____
_____

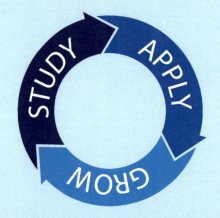

Determination (Faith) + Discipline = Growth

LESSON IX
KNOWING GOD'S WILL FOR YOUR LIFE

"Now this is the confidence that we have in Him, that if we ask anything according to His will, He hears us."
- I John 5:14

The most challenging aspect in a Christian's life is to know the Will of God for one's own life. How do you know for certain that what you are doing is God's Will?

The following are three steps, which will help you to know God's Will, and which will also keep you from falling into deception.

1. THE CHARACTER OF GOD

If someone told you that your best friend had said something negative about you, you would not believe it. This is because you have known your friend long enough, and know that he or she would never say something like that about you, because it is not his/her character to do so. Similarly, when you know God for who He is, you will not blame Him when something goes wrong in your life, because you know that it does not fit the Character of God.

> James 1:16-17
> *"Do not be deceived, my beloved brethren. (17) Every good gift and every perfect gift is from above, and comes down from the Father of lights, with whom there is no variation or shadow of turning."*

The Scriptures help us know God for who He is:

Exodus 34:6 (NIV)

_____

_____

I Peter 1:16

_____

_____

The one word that sums up the Character of God in I John 4:8

_____

Write down I Corinthians 13:4-7

_____

_____

Love is more than a feeling - love demonstrates character. If the choices you make are inconsistent with God's Character, then it is not the Will of God. Because God's Will will never contradict His Character.

2. THE WORD OF GOD

The Scripture is God's infallible Word to you and me; it is the inspired Word of God written under the inspiration of the Holy Spirit, and not man's opinion on life, or a book of good suggestions.

Just as you would not want to contradict your own word, in the same way, God will not contradict His Word.

The Word of God has already revealed His Will to you regarding your attitudes (motives), your choice of words and your conduct (behaviour). The Bible reveals the known Will of God.

Many Christians only want to know the Will of God concerning their jobs and marriage. This way of knowing God's Will is just for our convenience and not out of a sincere heart to embrace the Will of God in its totality for our lives.

Knowing God's Will should not be an event, but a way of life.

Write down the following verses concerning God's Will for your life.

1. Baptism with Holy Spirit - Luke 11:13

   _____

   _____

2. Your conversations - Ephesians 4:29

   _____

   _____

3. Worry/Anxiety - Matthew 6:31

   _____

   _____

4. Marriage - II Corinthians 6:14

   _____

   _____

5. Tithing - Malachi 3:10

   _____

   _____

6. Relationships - John 15:12

   _____

   _____

7. Forgiveness - Mark 11:25-26

   _____

   _____

8. Blessings - Hebrews 11:6

_____

_____

9. Health - James 5:14-15

_____

_____

10. Prosperity - III John Vs. 2

_____

_____

11. Studying the Word of God - II Timothy 2:15

_____

_____

12. Witnessing - Acts 1:8

_____

_____

Even as you have looked at this list, it is important to know that this is a matter of **your obedience**, because God has already revealed His Will in His Word concerning these areas in your life.

Our obedience to God's Word is a good place to start in seeing God's Will being established in our lives. When we walk in obedience to the **known** Will of God (the Word of God), it then becomes easy to know the **specific** Will of God in the other areas of our life (our career, our calling, marriage, etc.).

3. THE FRUIT OF LIFE AND PEACE

The Will of God will always lead you to life; the outcome will always be positive, and not negative. The Will of God will be a blessing to you, and will not harm you. It will draw you closer to God and not away from God.

Jeremiah 29:11
_____
_____

I am not saying that you won't have hardships, but through it all, you will have a quiet confidence in your spirit, knowing that God is with you.

> Isaiah 32:17-18 (NIV)
> "The fruit of that righteousness will be peace; its effect will be _____ and _____ forever. (18) My people will live in peaceful dwelling places, in secure homes, in undisturbed places of rest."

Lastly, the Peace of God in your spirit (not mind) is your guiding factor. Once you have made a decision in your heart, it will be advisable to see if the Peace of God in your heart still prevails. The Peace of God in your heart acts like an umpire; when you make a wrong decision, you will feel the absence of God's Peace in your heart. This is a good indicator to re-think your decision.

MY JOURNAL

"I still remember that sunny afternoon when I hopped onto a bus in Chennai (India), feeling confused and uncertain about my future. My head was hot, literally, with the intensity of the anxiety that I was going through because I had just received a strong letter from my Dad. His letter disapproved of my decision, saying, "You are not to go to Singapore to study". The little hope I had for a better college was soon vanishing. So, as I sat in the bus, I wondered what I would tell the person concerning my decision of going to Singapore, when the Holy Spirit spoke to me saying, "Stop listening to what is in your head. Listen to your spirit". I found that there was a peace in my spirit when I shut out all those thoughts of confusion, as if nothing was wrong. At that time, God drew my attention to Philippians 4:7 which says, "And the peace of God, which surpasses all understanding, will guard your hearts and minds through Christ Jesus".

It was the Peace of God in my heart that led me to find God's Will in my life.

I finally arrived at the person's home to give him my answer. I had to inform him of my decision. Do I tell him what my Dad said? Or do I tell him what I believe in my spirit? I decided to tell him that I was willing to pursue my studies in Singapore. In my heart, I said,

> *"Lord, only you will have to provide me with the money for my ticket to Singapore".*
>
> *I felt relieved after making that decision, and there was a sense of joy in my spirit (heart). I left the matter into God's Hands, awaiting what the outcome would be. A couple of weeks later, I got another letter from my Dad. With great curiosity, I opened the letter to see what he had to say. It was a jaw-dropping moment. I could hardly believe what he said in his letter. For the first time in my entire life I heard my Dad saying, "Son, I believe God is leading you. Go ahead with your studies in Singapore" - this had to be God!*
>
> *The most valuable lesson I learnt is to always listen to what the Peace of God is telling me in my spirit. Since then, the Peace of God has been the guiding factor in my life and ministry."*

Isn't it interesting to know that the Peace of God surpasses all our understanding. The word 'surpass' means 'exceed; be greater than'. In other words, there is a peace that God gives you that your mind cannot comprehend. This peace surpasses your human reasoning or understanding. Notice the verse says that the peace *"will guard your heart* (spirit) *and then your mind"* (Emphasis added). Most Christians look for a logical peace (understanding) in their mind where the circumstances suit them, instead of the peace of God in their spirit (heart).

Philippians 4:6 says, *"Be anxious for nothing, but in everything by prayer and supplication, with thanksgiving, let your requests be made known to God"*. After you have prayed and left what you were worrying about in God's hands, listen to what the peace of God is saying in your heart.

> Colossians 3:15
> *"And let the peace of God rule in your hearts, to which also you were called in one body; and be thankful."*

If you learn to listen to what God is speaking to you in your spirit, then you won't have to give in to your mind and emotions, which could steal your joy, disturb your relationships, and rob you of your victory.

Therefore, if you want to be established in the Will of God, your decisions must be in line with:
    1. The Character of God
    2. The Word of God
    3. The Peace of God

If your decision contradicts any one of the above three, then you may be deceived while trying to make the right decision.

I John 5:14-15 (NKJV)
"Now this is the confidence that we have in Him, that if we ask anything according to His will, He hears us. (15) And if we know that He hears us, whatever we ask, we know that we have the petitions that we have asked of Him."

PERSONAL REFLECTION

Identify the areas in your life which are not in line with the Will of God.

Choose appropriate Scriptures that will keep you focused on walking in the Will of God with regards to these specific areas of your life.

MEMORY VERSE

"And we know that all things work together for good to those who love God, to those who are the called according to His purpose."

Romans 8:28

GOAL

Live in the Known Will of God before you seek the Specific Will of God in your life.

REVIEW OF LESSON IX

What are the three main factors that you have learnt in this lesson that gives you the assurance that you are walking in the Will of God?

1. _____
2. _____
3. _____

Love is more than a feeling - love is _____.

Knowing God's Will should not be an event, but a _____.

The Peace of God surpasses _____ our understanding.

How did you apply Lesson IX in your life?
_____
_____

Write down the memory verse you learnt last week?
_____
_____

Determination (Faith) + Discipline = Growth

LESSON X
WHY FASTING?

" ... do not appear to men to be fasting, but to your Father who is in the secret place; and your Father who sees in secret will reward you openly".
- Matthew 6:18

Fasting has been a Biblical practice that originated in the Old Testament and continued in the New Testament. While He was on Earth, Jesus not only fasted but also validated fasting as a **spiritual discipline** for every Christian.

By nature, we live self-indulgent lives; we hardly deprive ourselves of the things we desire. More often than not, we keep giving in to these desires, which eventually lead us into bondage. The more we feed our carnal desires, the stronger will our cravings get.

Fasting is about starving the self-indulgent nature in us, so that we can be spiritually strong. It positions us to be in a spiritual place, where we can be in sync with God and His plans for our life.

Just as food helps one's physical body to grow and become strong, fasting and prayer help one to grow and become spiritually strong.

Jesus said in Matthew 6:17-18, *"But you, when you fast, anoint your head and wash your face, (18) so that you do not appear to men to be fasting, but to your Father who is in the _____ _____; and your Father who sees in secret will _____".*

Fasting requires us to set aside our time to align our thoughts, our will, our emotions and our spirit, with what God wants, **and not the other way round.** People, especially in the religious circles, use fasting as a means for God to align Himself to their plans and their desires - this is not the Biblical purpose of fasting. Jesus rebuked the people for taking on a religious practice of fasting, which was done more out of a routine to impress people, rather than for them to grow spiritually with God.

Jesus used the word *"when"* you fast and not 'if' you fast, indicating that we **should** give ourselves to prayer and fasting from time-to-time. He also said in verse 17, *"when you fast in secret* (a time alone with God), *and pray, Your Heavenly Father sees you in secret and rewards you openly"* (Emphasis added).

Fasting not only aligns us with God's plan and purposes, but it also positions us in a place, where He can reward us. Every time we fast, we should be strengthened in our faith and not be discouraged. The discipline of fasting enables us to hear from God; and when we hear God speak, it gives us hope and direction for whatever we are trusting God for.

ISAIAH 58 SPELLS OUT FOR US GOD'S CHOSEN FAST

The people of Israel accused God saying, *"Why have we fasted ... and You have not seen? Why have we afflicted our souls, and You take no notice?"* (Isaiah 58:3). They were disappointed because God had not answered their prayers despite all their religious fasting.

God spoke to His people through Isaiah the Prophet saying, *"Your fasting ends in quarrelling and strife, and in striking each other with wicked fists. You cannot fast as you do today _____."* - Isaiah 58:4 (NIV)

In verse 5, God questioned their motive of fasting by provoking them to think, *"Is this the kind of fast I have chosen, only a day for people to humble themselves? Is it only for bowing one's head like a reed and for lying in sackcloth and ashes? Is that what you call a fast, a day acceptable to the Lord?"* In the Old Testament, when people fasted, they bowed their heads down like a reed, and would lie in sackcloth and ashes because these were considered as the outward signs of repentance and of humbling one's self before God - their purpose of fasting was to humble themselves only for that day ... and we fall into the same trap as the people of that day.

It is for this reason that God asked them, *"Is that what you call a fast, a day acceptable to the Lord?"* (Isaiah 58:5b)

From verse 6 onwards, we see God correcting their motives to fast. The Chapter of 'Isaiah 58' is commonly known as 'God's Chosen Fast'.

> Isaiah 58:6-7
> *"Is this not the fast that I have chosen: to loose the bonds of wickedness, to undo the heavy burdens, to let the oppressed go free, and that you break every yoke? (7) Is it not to share your bread with the hungry, and that you bring to your house the poor who are cast out; when you see the naked, that you cover him, and not hide yourself from your own flesh?"*

The word 'oppression', means 'prolonged cruel or unjust treatment or exercise of authority'. It is in this context that Jesus uses the word oppressed, to indicate that people were suffering and were under the Devil's authority, which caused sickness, disease, poverty and conflict (For example - Acts 10:38).

God sees people in this World held in chains, both in the physical as well as in the spiritual realm. He sees the injustice, the bondage and the oppression that the Devil uses to keep people bound. Fasting gives us an aerial view of how God sees the World. So, when you view people in this light, you begin to understand why Jesus confronted the Devil ... to see people saved, delivered and healed.

The word 'yolk' can be used in both a negative and positive context. But in this verse, it refers to something that is negative and has attached itself to a person, and which needs to be broken. This yolk can refer to man's sinful ways (addictions), ungodly relationships that people are tied too, etc., that keep them in bondage.

So, what did Jesus do? He fulfilled the mandate of God's chosen fast. When you fast with the purpose of seeking God's desire, you in-turn begin to seek after God's Kingdom and His righteousness. Jesus said in Matthew 6, *"But seek first the kingdom of God and His righteousness, and all these things shall be added to you"*

Fasting helps you to place God's agenda above your agenda, and His plan for your life above your plans. Placing God's plans above your plans and agendas may seem difficult, but trust me, God definitely knows what is best for you. He offers you a life that is worth living.

REWARDS OF GOD'S CHOSEN FAST IN ISAIAH 58 (AMPC)

- *"Then shall your light break forth like the morning ... "* (Verse 8a) - If you are going through or a period of uncertainties or in a place of oppression, symbolically this is a season of darkness. But the reward of fasting positions you to be in a place, where there will be a sudden break-through, like the brilliance of the light that shines forth at the breaking of dawn - a new beginning.

- *" ... your healing shall spring forth speedily ... "* (Verse 8b) - Healing is about restoration and wholeness. Fasting positions us to be in a place, where we can receive physical healing, emotional healing, and most importantly, the healing of our beliefs speedily.

- *" ... your righteousness shall go before you ... "* (Verse 8c) - When you fast according to Isaiah 58, your righteousness, referring to who you are and what you do, will bring you to a place of experiencing uncommon favour from both God and man. Jesus spoke about this in Matthew 5:16, *"Let your light so shine before men, that they may see your good works and glorify your Father in heaven"*. In Isaiah 58:10, the Bible goes on to speak about us giving our lives to serve God and people.

"And if you pour out that with which you sustain your own life for the hungry and satisfy the need of the afflicted, then shall your light rise in darkness, and your obscurity and gloom become like the noonday"

The words *"obscurity"* and *"gloom"*, refer to insignificance and a lack of purpose. On the other hand, *"noon day"* is just the opposite of obscurity and gloom. When you live your life satisfying the needs of the afflicted, then shall your light rise in darkness. God's way of rewarding us is to bring us out from a place of gloom and insignificance, to a place of recognition and significance (noon day).

- *" ... the glory of the Lord shall be your rear guard (Verse 8d)"* - This speaks of God being your Protector. The Glory of God is the Character of God; in other words, you can always count on God, knowing that at all times He will protect and sustain you.

- In Psalm 23:6, the Psalmist knew Jesus as his Shepherd, that he said, *"Surely goodness and mercy shall follow me **all the days of my life** ..."*. He knew that no matter what the circumstances were, he could always fall back on the mercy and goodness of God, knowing that God was his rear guard.

- *"Then you shall call, and the Lord will answer; you shall cry, and He will say, Here I am."* (Verse 9) - This is one of my favourite rewards. This verse starts with *"Then"*, indicating the pre-requisite regarding fasting. When you fast God's way, it is only then you can live in the assurance of this reward - that whenever you call on God, He will answer; when you cry, He will say, *"Here I am"*. What a privilege!

- *" ... the Lord shall guide you continually and satisfy you ... you shall be like a watered garden and like a spring of water whose waters fail not"* (Verse 11) - The Lord promises to guide you always and to satisfy your needs. When fasting becomes a lifestyle, you can expect God to guide you continually. His guidance will always lead you to a place of being satisfied and living a fulfilled life. The Bible paints a picture of us living our lives like a well-watered garden (always beautiful), and like a spring whose waters never fail (a sense of hope and life).

- *" ... your ancient ruins shall be rebuilt; you shall raise up the foundations of [buildings that have laid waste for] many generations ... "* (Verse 12) - Fasting not only changes you, but it also changes your purpose. When you fast God's way, He will use you to build up the foundations that will impact generations to come. These foundations are physical (service to the poor and afflicted), spiritual (the ministry of reconciliation to God) and moral (bring people to a place of living Godly lives).

Fasting does not change God; it changes us and transforms the way we live.

Read Isaiah 58:9-10, and write down what can hinder you from fasting effectively.

_____

_____

THE BIBLE TALKS ABOUT THREE TYPES OF FASTING:

A REGULAR FAST

Traditionally, a regular fast is about refraining from eating all food. Most people drink water or juice during a regular fast. When Jesus fasted in the desert, the Bible says in Matthew 4:2, *"And when He had fasted _____ and _____, afterward He was hungry."*

This verse tells us that Jesus refrained from eating completely for 40 days and nights. At the end of His fast, the Bible mentions that Jesus was hungry, not thirsty.

I often hear about people going on long periods of fasting. I believe that Jesus is our example, and He has set for us the limits of how many days our fast should last.

A FULL FAST

This fast is about abstaining from food and drink and was practiced only by those who received a direct instruction from the Lord. In Acts 9:9, Paul went on a full fast for three days after he had an encounter with Jesus on the road to Damascus - *"For three days he was blind, and did not eat or drink anything"*.

Esther also called for this type of fast in Esther 4:15-16 (NIV) - *"Then Esther sent this reply to Mordecai: 'Go, gather together all the Jews who are in Susa, and fast for me. _____ _____. When this is done, I will go to the king, even though it is against the law. And if I perish, I perish'."*

> **Note:**
> It is recommended that this type of fast be done with extreme caution, and if you do so, it should not be for an extended period of time. It is advisable to stick to the regular type of fast unless God specifically instructs you to do so otherwise. Remember, the effectiveness of a fast is in you being spiritually tuned to God and not just abstaining from eating or drinking.

A PARTIAL FAST

This fast is about you **feeding your hunger and not your appetite.** Most of us eat to feed our appetites and not because we are hungry.

In Daniel 10:2-3, the Bible says that when Daniel fasted he ate no _____ food, no _____ or _____.

In Daniel 1:12, they restricted their diet to vegetables and water - *"Please test your servants for ten days: Give us nothing but vegetables to eat and water to drink"*.

MY JOURNAL

"I learnt about fasting by giving myself to the discipline of fasting. My first few years of fasting were very depressing. I would fast only because God had instructed us to do so in His Word. Later on, I was motivated to fast only because I wanted to see God answer my prayers or because I wanted to have a supernatural encounter with God. But, it greatly discouraged me when none of the above happened. Something was not right with the way I fasted, because it left me more discouraged than encouraged. Until one day, when I meditated on what Jesus had said in Matthew 6 - "when you fast God sees you in secret and rewards you openly". At that moment, I felt God suddenly turn on a light inside of me. For the first time, I saw where I had gone wrong."

So, from that day onwards, every time I broke my fast, I would live in the anticipation of God answering my prayers. And when I fasted this way for the very first time, I saw a vision of God calling me into Ministry.

You are fasting in faith, and not in doubt.
First of all, I began to see how much faith I had lacked to actually believe that God not only saw me, but He also heard me when I sought Him in secret. Today, I consider this as one of the greatest rewards of fasting (Isaiah 58).

We can eradicate doubt when we begin to believe that God has heard our prayer. Every time you pray, it is good to remind yourself that God sees you and He pays heed to your prayers.

Your reward comes after the fast and not during the fast.
Secondly, I understood that at the end of our fast, we should be more positive and hopeful of what God has promised, because Jesus said the Father would reward us openly.

Irrespective of what we are fasting for, we must always seek the Will of God in that matter, and we must be open to God's divine guidance. Almost every miracle in the Bible occurred because people heard God and obeyed what He had instructed them to do.

Fasting is a spiritual discipline that helps us hear God speaking to us.

Practical Steps to Fasting

1. Align your heart/desires/plans with God's Heart and plan for you.
2. Declare your intentions before God.
3. Spend time meditating on the Word of God.
4. Ask God for His ability to sustain you during your fast.
5. When you break your fast, break with faith and thanksgiving, knowing that God will reward you for what you prayed for.

PERSONAL REFLECTION

When and why was the last time you fasted?

_____

_____

MEM👁RY VERSE

"…so that you do not appear to men to be fasting, but to your Father who is in the secret place; and your Father who sees in secret will reward you openly".

Mathew 6:18

PLUMBLINE

GAL

Make fasting and prayer a spiritual discipline in your life.

REVIEW OF LESSON X

While He was on Earth, Jesus not only fasted but also validated fasting as a _____ _____ for every Christian.

Fasting requires us to set aside our time to align our _____, our _____, our _____ and our _____, with what God wants,

Fasting does not change God; it _____ us and _____ the way we live.

How did you apply Lesson X in your life?
_____
_____

Write down the memory verse you learnt last week?
_____
_____

Determination (Faith) + Discipline = Growth

ANSWERS

The following pages contain the answers to this Workbook's various exercises from all the Lessons. For the Scripture verses which need to be filled in, we encourage you to go through your Bible and write them down.

LESSON I
A NEW BEGINNING

James 1:16
Every good
every perfect
variation

John 3:5
water
Spirit

We can only enter into God's Kingdom by the work of the Word of God and the Holy Spirit.

REVIEW OF LESSON I

What are the two spiritual Kingdoms?
1. Kingdom of God
2. Kingdom of Satan

What are the two things that you need to be consistent with, in order to grow in any aspect of your life?
1. Determination
2. Discipline

LESSON II
THE BELT OF TRUTH
PART I
THE TRUTH ABOUT THE BIBLE AND GOD

Ephesians 6:14
truth

Write down the names of all the books in the New Testament under each section:
The Gospels:
(4) - Matthew, Mark, Luke, John

Books of History:
(1) - Acts of the Apostles

Letters to the Church:
(21) - Romans, Corinthians (I and II), Galatians, Ephesians, Philippians, Colossians, Thessalonians (I and II), Timothy (I and II), Titus, Philemon, Hebrews, James, Peter (I and II), John (I, II and III), Jude

Prophecy:
(1) - Revelation

REVIEW OF LESSON II (PART I)

What are the five characteristics of God that you have learnt in this lesson?
God is:
- Compassionate
- Gracious
- Slow to anger
- Abounds in Love
- Faithful

LESSON II
THE BELT OF TRUTH
PART II
BELIEF ABOUT YOURSELF AND OTHERS

Ephesians 4:23-24
renewed
new man

In the following verses, write down your responsibility towards one another:
Colossians 3:13
Forgive one another.

Mark 11:25
Forgive one another.

Read James 2:1-3, and write down the one thing that we should not do with regards to those who are poor?
We should not be partial.

In today's context, how would you apply what Galatians 3:28 says?
All of us are one in the eyes of Jesus.

Exodus 20:3-4
have no other gods
not make for yourself a carved image

Exodus 20:7
the name of the Lord your God in vain

Exodus 20:8-10
the Sabbath day

Exodus 20:12
Honour your father and your mother

Ephesians 6:2-3
1. That it may be well with you
2. You may live long on the Earth

Exodus 20:13
murder
Exodus 20:14

adultery

Exodus 20:15
steal

Exodus 20:16
bear false witness

Exodus 20:17
not covet

How does the New Testament sum up all the 10 commandants in Romans 13:9?
" ... are all summed up in this saying, namely, 'You shall love your neighbor as yourself'."

REVIEW OF LESSON II (PART II)

God no longer looks at you as a sinner, but as <u>righteous</u> because you are in Christ.

Your <u>spiritual</u> identity is our true identity.

Most of our obedience towards God is worked out in our relationships with others.

What are the 2 commandments that Jesus gave us to keep?
1. To love God
2. To love one another

LESSON III
THE BREASTPLATE OF RIGHTEOUSNESS

Hebrews 10:10
once for all

Believing is with the <u>heart</u> and confession is with the <u>mouth.</u>

When we confess our sin before God, He is <u>faithful</u> and <u>just</u> to <u>forgive</u> us our sins and to <u>cleanse</u> us from all unrighteousness.

What do I confess with my mouth?
I confess what Jesus accomplished for me on the Cross - He died for my sins.

What do I do with my heart?
Believe.

We must learn to <u>receive</u> His forgiveness by <u>faith</u>.

… the Bible says, that God is faithful and just to <u>cleanse</u> us from all unrighteousness.

Why should you to abide in The Vine?
To bear much fruit - without Him I can do nothing.

II Corinthians 1:20
in Him
are Yes
in Him Amen

REVIEW OF LESSON III

Sin is not the presence of evil, but the absence of God's Holiness.

Write down what are the two kinds of righteousness that the Bible talks about?
1. A righteousness that is derived by following specific rules and laws in a ritualistic manner.
2. A righteousness that comes by faith.

How do you receive your forgiveness?
By faith.

The basis for which God answers our prayer is not based on our righteousness, but on His righteousness.

LESSON IV
THE GOSPEL OF PEACE
PART I
UNDERSTANDING OUR MISSION

Ephesians 3:12
boldness
access
confidence

This peace that Jesus came to bring is peace with <u>God,</u> peace with <u>ourselves</u> and peace with others.

II Corinthians 5:18
ministry

II Timothy 2:20-23
foolish
ignorant

Matthew 5:13-16
salt
light
Let your light

What are the three signs that follow a person who believes in Christ?
1. Cast out demons
2. Speak with new tongues
3. Lay hands on the sick and they will recover

REVIEW OF LESSON IV (PART I)

Having been reconciled with God, what is the ministry that you have been chosen for? (II Corinthians 5:18)
Ministry of Reconciliation.

God wants us to yield our bodies as instruments of <u>righteousness</u>, so that He could fulfil His plans through us.

Why should our feet be prepared with the Gospel of Peace?
God wants to heal and deliver those who are suffering and those who are in bondage, and He wants to eradicate poverty and corruption, but, He can only accomplish this task through you and I.

LESSON IV
THE GOSPEL OF PEACE
PART II
ESTABLISHING YOURSELF IN THE GOSPEL

Romans 1:16
believes

John 3:16-17
believes
condemn
saved

Romans 3:23
all

Isaiah 59:1-2 (NIV)
not

I Timothy 2:5
one

Hebrews 10:17-18
no more

John 14:6
No one

John 10:9
anyone

REVIEW OF LESSON IV (PART II)

What are the five main aspects of the Gospel?
1. God loves you even when you were a sinner
2. Sin separates you from God
3. Jesus is God's only provision for your sin
4. Jesus is alive and He is the only way to God
5. You must know God personally

LESSON V
THE SHIELD OF FAITH

I Thessalonians 3:5
tempter
tempted

Who is able to keep you from falling?
Jesus

I Peter 2:23 (NIV)
entrusted himself to him

According to Hebrews 4, who is your High Priest?
Jesus

What does He do when we are tempted?
_____
_____

How should we approach the Throne of Grace?
boldly

What do you receive?
_____
_____

REVIEW OF LESSON V

According to Hebrews 4:14, what does Jesus do?
Jesus intercedes for us.

And what is our responsibility?
We need to hold fast to our confession.

<u>Faith</u> in Jesus is our shield that nullifies the fiery darts of the enemy.

LESSON VI
THE HELMET OF SALVATION

Write down the two things you must do when faced with temptation.
1. Take the negative thought captive
2. Divert my thoughts onto something positive

REVIEW OF LESSON VI

The assurance of your salvation and our forgiveness is not based on your feelings, but is based on what <u>God's Word</u> says.

The purpose for the Helmet of Salvation is to <u>guard our thought life</u> from thoughts of fear, hatred, unbelief, thoughts of lust, etc..

Sin is first <u>conceived</u> in our mind before it becomes an action.

LESSON VII
THE SWORD OF THE SPIRIT

Matthew 4
Verse 3
tempter

Verse 4
"It is written"

Verse 7
"It is written again"

Revelation 3:5
overcomes

I Corinthians 10:12
fall

Ephesians 3:12
boldness
access

Proverbs 18:21
tongue

REVIEW OF LESSON VII

I need to gird myself with the <u>Belt of Truth</u>, knowing who my Heavenly Father is, wear the <u>Breastplate of Righteousness</u>, because I am made righteous in Christ. My feet should be equipped with the <u>Gospel of Peace</u> to be effective in sharing the Gospel of Salvation. I must always use the <u>Shield of Faith</u> to protect me from the plots and plans of the enemy. The <u>Helmet of Salvation</u> is what protects me from doubt and temptations. And above all, the <u>Sword of the Spirit</u> which is the Word of God enables me to walk in victory!

LESSON VIII
DEVOTIONAL LIFE

I Corinthians 1:9
faithful
fellowship

Matthew 7:11
how much more
give good things

Luke 22:39-40 (NIV)
as usual

Luke 5:16
often

Hebrews 11:6
must believe that He is
rewarder
Him

Hebrews 13:15
continually
lips

Hebrews 4:16 (NIV)
confidence
receive

James 4:2
ask

I Peter 5:7
cares

Read Mathew 6:25-34 and write down the things that your Heavenly Father does not want you to worry about.
1. Life
2. Food
3. Drink
4. Clothing

Mark 11:22-25 (ESV)

not doubt
believes
believe that you have received it

Philippians 4:6 (ESV)
anything
supplication
thanksgiving

Luke 10:38-42
What did Mary do?
Sat at Jesus' Feet and heard His Word

What prevented Martha from spending time with Jesus?
Her worries and anxieties - being distracted/pre-occupied with much serving.

What did Jesus say about Mary?
Jesus said that there was only one thing that was needed and that Mary has chosen that good part and it would not be taken away from her.

What time and place of the day did Jesus choose to spend time alone with His Father?
Time - *Very early in the morning* (Mark 1:35)
Place - *A solitary* (Mark 1:35) *lonely place* (Luke 5:16) - *Mount of Olives* (Luke 22:39)

According to Psalm 5:3, when is a good time to meet with the Lord each day?
In the morning

Proverbs 3:5-7 (NIV)
and He will direct your paths straight

The three steps that guarantee God guiding you are:
all
your own
all
Him

Psalm 16:11
path

Romans 4:20-21 (NIV)
unbelief
faith
persuaded

Matthew 7:24
puts them into practice
wise man

Joshua 1:8
mouth
meditate
observe

Psalm 119:11
heart
sin

REVIEW OF LESSON VIII

Jesus died so that our <u>relationship</u> and <u>fellowship</u> with God was restored.

The only thing that pleases our Heavenly Father is <u>faith</u>

Whenever God speaks to you through His Word, you must <u>act</u> on what you hear.

Write down the benefits that you have by spending time with God.
- To get direction from God
- To become more like God
- To grow in faith
- For wisdom
- For prosperity and success
- For victory over sin

LESSON IX
KNOWING GOD'S WILL FOR YOUR LIFE

The one word that sums up the Character of God in I John 4:8
Love :)

Isaiah 32:17-18 (NIV)
quietness
confidence

REVIEW OF LESSON IX

What are the three main factors that you have learnt in this lesson that gives you the assurance that you are walking in the Will of God?
- The Character of God
- The Word of God
- The Fruit of Life and Peace (The Peace of God)

Love is more than a feeling - love is <u>character</u>.

Knowing God's Will should not be an event, but a <u>way of life</u>.

The Peace of God surpasses <u>all</u> our understanding.

LESSON X
WHY FASTING?

Matthew 6:17-18
secret place
reward you openly

Isaiah 58:4 (NIV)
and expect your voice to be heard on high

Read Isaiah 58:9-10, and write down what can hinder you from fasting effectively
- *The yoke of oppression* (exploiting people)
- *The pointing finger* (accusing people)
- *Malicious talk* (gossip)

A Regular Fast
Matthew 4:2
forty days
forty nights

A Full Fast
Esther 4:15-16 (NIV)
" ... *Do not eat or drink for three days, night or day. I and my attendants will fast as you do* ..."

A Partial Fast
Daniel 10:2-3
pleasant
meat
wine

REVIEW OF LESSON X

While He was on Earth, Jesus not only fasted but also validated fasting as a spiritual discipline for every Christian.

Fasting requires us to set aside our time to align our thoughts, our will, our emotions and our spirit, with what God wants,

Fasting does not change God; it changes us and transforms the way we live.

EVALUATE YOUR PROGRESS

"He who overcomes shall be clothed in white garments, and I will not blot out his name from the Book of Life; but I will confess his name before My Father and before His angels".
- Revelation 3:5

Everything that God created has the ability to grow and produce life. You were destined for progress, and not stagnation. Progress is about growing, which is often measured by the goals we have achieved. The basic requirements needed to achieve anything are 'Determination' and 'Discipline' to study and apply what you have learnt. Having come to the end of this workbook, you can now evaluate your growth by seeing if you have achieved the following goals.

(On a scale of 1-10)

1. Are you involved in a local Church in a meaningful way? _____
2. Do you have a Biblical view/perspective about God, yourself and others? _____
3. Is your faith based on God's righteousness for you? _____
4. How often have you shared the Gospel with others? _____
5. Have you been able to overcome the temptations that have come your way? _____
6. Are you able to guard your thoughts? _____
7. Have you cultivated the habit of spending time with God and His Word daily? _____
8. Are you able to trust God with your anxieties? _____
9. Are you walking in the Will of God concerning the different aspects of your life? _____
10. Have you made fasting one of your spiritual disciplines? _____

For you to continually grow and walk in victory, I would encourage you to review the lessons and apply the appropriate goals for your life.

Growing is a process, and some people grow in their spiritual lives faster than others. Your determination and your discipline to study and apply God's Word will cause you to live an overcomer's life. If you are still struggling in certain areas of your life, please do not give up. Remember you are in a spiritual battle and Jesus is on your side.

Use your own creative way to remind yourself of what you want to achieve; for example, write down your goals on your screensaver, or be accountable to someone, etc. - this will help you to walk in victory.

Revelation 3:21
"To him who overcomes I will grant to sit with Me on My throne, as I also overcame and sat down with My Father on His throne."